FAT-FREE HOLIDAY RECIPES

Low-fat and fat-free meal plans for traditional family celebrations and get-togethers including Christmas, Thanksgiving, New Year's Day, Easter, Hanukkah, Passover, and much more

SANDRA WOODRUFF, RD

Avery Publishing Group

Garden City Park, New York

Text Illustrator: John Wincek
Interior Color Photographs: John Strange
Front Cover Photograph: Envision/Steven Mark Needham
Back Cover Photographs: John Strange
Cover Design: William Gonzalez
Typesetting: Bonnie Freid
In-House Editor: Joanne Abrams

This Premium Edition was adapted from the original full edition available from
Avery Publishing Group, Inc.
120 Old Broadway
Garden City Park, NY 11040
516-741-2155

Cataloging-in-Publication Data

Woodruff, Sandra L.
Fat-free holiday recipes : delicious fat-free and low-fat
recipes for holidays, family celebrations, and elegant
get-togethers / Sandra Woodruff
p. cm.
Includes index.
ISBN 0-89529-629-2

1. Holiday cookery.   2. Low-fat----Recipes.   I. Title.
TX739.W66 1995641.5'68
QB194-1766

Contents

Preface

As a nutritionist, I have long been aware of the need to help people eliminate fat from their diet. I also know the importance of creating nutrient-rich dishes made with whole grains and other ingredients that are as close as possible to their natural state. And because of my work as a teacher, I also know that foods must be more than just healthy. They must be visually appealing and absolutely delicious. If not, people simply won't eat them.

Fat-Free Holiday Recipes is the perfect book for people who want to reduce the fat in their diet, maximize their nutrition, and treat their friends and family to delicious holiday and special-occasion dishes. From Spicy Barbecue Meatballs to Creamy Cucumber Dip to Chocolate Raspberry Torte, every recipe has been designed to reduce fat and boost nutrition. Just as important, every recipe has been kitchen-tested to make sure that you enjoy success each and every time you make it, and people-tested to make sure that every dish you create is sure to be a hit.

Fat-Free Holiday Recipes begins by explaining just why dietary fat should be reduced, and just how much fat is allowable in a healthy diet. You'll also learn of the many nonfat and low-fat ingredients that will help you reduce fat without reducing taste, and you'll learn about the nutritional analysis that accompanies each and every recipe in the book.

Following this important information, the book is divided into four parts, each of which focuses on a specific type of party or holiday food, or presents complete menus and recipes for special-occasion meals. Part One offers a cornucopia of low-fat and fat-free finger-food recipes that are perfect for any gathering. Included in this section are recipes for both hot treats, like meatballs and kabobs, and cold treats, like finger sandwiches and dips. Also included are recipes for hot and cold beverages that round out party menus and add to the festivities without adding fat.

Part Two presents menus and accompanying recipes for five traditional holidays, including Thanksgiving, Christmas, Hanukkah, Passover, and Easter. Each menu is composed of a variety of taste-tempting fat-free and low-fat appetizers, main dishes, side dishes, and desserts. Whenever possible, options have been provided to allow you to tailor the meal to suit your family's tastes. The Thanksgiving menu, for instance, gives you a selection of stuffings, cranberry sauces, and side dishes----in addition to the turkey, of course. In many menus, you'll find low-fat and no-fat versions of traditional holiday foods. In others, you'll find new and exciting recipes for dishes that may become new holiday traditions in your home. Best of all, each menu includes suggested plan-ahead strategies that will allow you to complete many of your preparations in advance, helping you avoid a last-minute rush on the day of your get-together.

Part Three presents our collection of holiday and party recipes with a bonanza of fat-free and low-fat dessert and baked-goods recipes. Whether you're searching for a festive quick bread to complement a simple luncheon dish or a dazzling grand finale to a special-occasion dinner, this section will meet your needs. All sweet treats are made without butter, margarine, or oil, and all are so delectable, no one but you will guess just how wholesome they are.

It is my hope that *Fat-Free Holiday Recipes* will prove to you, as well as to your friends and family, that party food does not have to be rich and fattening, and that low-fat food can be satisfying, exciting, and fun. So eat well and enjoy! As you will see, it is possible to do both----every day of the year.

Introduction

Great food adds that special touch to any occasion. Food livens up a party and makes every holiday more enjoyable and memorable. Unfortunately, holidays and parties have long been thought of as a license to indulge in fat, sugar, and salt----ingredients that we now know must be kept to a minimum in a healthful diet. The good news is that the wide availability of low-fat and nonfat products, as well as a greater knowledge of healthy cooking techniques, now means that *good* doesn't have to be *greasy*. Moreover, elegant and delicious dishes that are special enough for any occasion can be just as easy to prepare as traditional special-occasion foods.

As a nutritionist and teacher, I began looking for ways to reduce or totally eliminate dietary fat a long time before anyone heard the term "fat-free." Through years of experimentation and kitchen testing, and with the help of clients and students, I have developed simple ways to do just that. Of course, because of our new awareness of the link between diet and health, many low-fat cookbooks are now available. Unfortunately, these cookbooks don't always use the most healthful ingredients. Often, artificial sweeteners and other highly processed ingredients are used to cut fat and calories. In the process, nutrition is often compromised. Moreover, these books often ignore an important part of everyone's life----holiday gatherings and special-occasion get-togethers. *Fat-Free Holiday Recipes* was designed to fill the gap by providing tried-and-true recipes that will enable you to create healthful, delicious low- and no-fat party menus.

The recipes in this book are far more than just low-fat or no-fat. Besides eliminating or greatly reducing fat, I have improved the nutritional value of recipes by using natural sweeteners like fruits and juices whenever possible. Whole grains and whole grain flours have also been used, providing added fiber and nutritional value. As an added bonus, the use of herbs, spices, and seasonings, as well as a minimal reliance on processed foods, has helped to keep sodium under control.

Probably the best part of these recipes, though, is their simplicity. Every effort has been made to keep the number of ingredients, pots, pans, and utensils to a minimum. This will save you time and make cleanup a breeze----important considerations for most people today.

At this point, you may be wondering why you

should even worry about what you eat during the holidays. After all, an occasional overindulgence will not ruin an otherwise healthy diet. But with great-tasting low-fat holiday favorites just as easy to prepare as their high-fat counterparts, why would you *not* opt for healthier alternatives? Besides, through the years, I've found that once people make the change to a low-fat diet, they really do prefer the fresher, lighter taste of foods made without fat----every day of the year.

As you will see, watching your fat intake does not have to mean feeling deprived during holidays and special occasions. In fact, this book is filled with ideas for easy and elegant entertaining, whether you are just having a few people over for coffee or holding an open house for fifty. From New Year's Day all the way to Christmas and Hanukkah, this book will help you begin new and exciting holiday traditions. I wish you the best of luck and health with all your fat-free cooking!

Getting the Fat Out of Parties

Do you dread social gatherings, fearing what they might do to your intentions to eat well? If so, you may have good reason. It is not uncommon for people to gain ten or even fifteen pounds between the start of the football season and New Year's Eve.

Food and festivity are part of the American way. Food does liven up a party, and there is nothing wrong with enjoying special dishes on special occasions. Unfortunately, traditional party favorites top the list of foods high in fat, sugar, and salt. Fatty dips, spreads, meats, cheeses, crackers, and chips are often the only selections on hors d'oeuvres tables. Have a taste of each, and you could easily consume a full day's worth of fat and calories. Most people fare no better at dinner parties, where the hosts go all out with a fat-laced gourmet menu. After all, it is a party, and your hosts want to serve "the best" to their guests.

Fortunately, many people now realize that delicious, appealing foods do not have to be loaded with fatty ingredients like cream, butter, and egg yolks. Nor does a large portion of meat have to be the centerpiece of a special-occasion meal. Elegant desserts, too, can be prepared with little or no fat, and with a lot less sugar than is usually used. That is why *Fat-Free Holiday Recipes* was written. In these pages, you will find a wide variety of simple and elegant hors d'oeuvres and dinner dishes made with nonfat and low-fat ingredients. You will be delighted by "defatted" versions of old favorites, as well as tempting new creations that will let you party to your heart's content.

Perhaps just as important, this book will show you that contrary to popular belief, putting together a party does not have to be an ordeal. As you will see, the recipes in this book will save you not only fat and calories, but also time and effort. Most of the recipes are very simple to follow, even for beginners, and are designed to create as little mess as possible, saving you cleanup time. The party menus even provide strategies for preparing foods in advance, so that little work will be required at the last minute, allowing you to enjoy your own party.

This section will explain why dietary fat should be decreased, and will guide you in budgeting your daily fat intake. In addition, we'll look at the various healthful ingredients used throughout this book----ingredients that will enable you to prune fat from every meal of the day, as well as from party foods and holiday feasts.

BIG FAT PROBLEMS

Excess fat may well be the number-one dietary problem in America. With more than twice the calories of carbohydrates and protein, fat is a concentrated source of calories. Compare a cup of butter or margarine (almost pure fat) with a cup of flour (almost pure carbohydrates). The butter has 1,600 calories, while the flour has only 400 calories. It's easy to see where most of our calories come from.

Besides being high in calories, fat is also readily converted into body fat when eaten in excess. Carbohydrate-rich foods eaten in excess are also stored as fat, but they must first be converted into fat----a process that burns up some of the carbohydrates. The bottom line is that a high-fat diet will cause 20 percent more weight gain than will a high-carbohydrate diet, even when the two diets contain the same number of calories. So a high-fat diet is a double-edged sword for the weight-conscious person. It is high in calories, and it is high in the kind of nutrient that is most readily stored as body fat.

But high-fat diets pose a threat to much more than our weight. When fatty diets lead to obesity, diseases like diabetes and high blood pressure can result. And specific types of fats present their own unique problems. For example, eating too much saturated fat----found in meat, butter, and palm and coconut oils, among other foods----raises blood cholesterol levels, setting the stage for heart disease. Polyunsaturated fat, once thought to be the solution to heart disease, can also be harmful when eaten in excess. A diet overly rich in corn oil, safflower oil, and other foods high in polyunsaturates can alter body chemistry to favor the development of blood clots, high blood pressure, and inflammatory diseases. Too much polyunsaturated fat can also promote free-radical damage in cells, contributing to heart disease and cancer.

Where do monounsaturated fats fit in? Monounsaturated fats----found in olive oil, canola oil, avocados, and nuts----have no known harmful effects other than being a concentrated source of calories, as all fats are.

Considering the problems caused by excess fat, you may think that it would be best to totally eliminate fat from your diet. But the fact is that we do need some dietary fat. For instance, linoleic acid, a polyunsaturated fat naturally present in grains, nuts, and seeds, is essential for life. The average adult needs a minimum of 3 to 6 grams of linoleic acid per day----the amount present in 1 to 2 teaspoonfuls of polyunsaturated vegetable oil or 1 to 2 tablespoonfuls of nuts and seeds. Linolenic acid, a fat found mainly in fish and green plants, is also essential for good health.

Unfortunately, many people are getting too much of a good thing. The liberal use of foods like mayonnaise, oil-based salad dressings, margarine, and cooking oils has created an unhealthy overdose of linoleic acid in the American diet. And, of course, most people also eat far too much saturated fat. How can we correct this? We can minimize the use of refined vegetable oils and table fats, and eat a diet rich in whole grains, fruits, and vegetables, with moderate amounts of nuts and seeds. This is what *Fat-Free Holiday Recipes* is all about. In the remainder of this section, you'll learn how to budget your daily fat intake, and you'll become acquainted with the healthful foods that will help you prune the fat from your diet and maximize the nutrients. Throughout the rest of the book, you'll learn how to use these foods to create sure-fire crowd pleasers for every holiday from January to December.

BUDGETING YOUR FAT

For most people, close to 40 percent of the calories in their diet come from fat. However, currently it is recommended that fat calories constitute no more than 30 percent of the diet, and, in fact, 20 to 25 percent would be even better in most cases. So the amount of fat you can eat every day is based on the number of calories you need. Because people's caloric needs depend on their weight, age, sex, activity level, and metabolic rate, these needs vary greatly among people. Most adults, though, must consume 13 to 15 calories per pound to maintain their weight. Of course, some people need even fewer calories, while very physically active people need more.

Once you have determined your calorie requirement, you can estimate a fat budget for yourself. Suppose you are a moderately active person who weighs 150 pounds. You will probably need about 15 calories per pound to maintain your weight, or about 2,250 per day. To limit your fat intake to 20 percent of your caloric intake, you can eat no more than 450 calories derived from fat per day (2,250 x .20 = 450). To convert this into grams of fat, divide by 9, as one gram of fat has 9 calories. Therefore, you should limit yourself to 50 grams of fat per day (450 ÷ 9 = 50).

The table at the bottom of this page shows both 20-percent and 25-percent maximum daily fat gram budgets. If you are overweight or underweight, go by the weight you would like to be. And keep in mind that although you have budgeted X amount of fat grams per day, you don't *have* to eat that amount of fat----you just have to avoid going over budget.

ABOUT THE INGREDIENTS

Never before has it been so easy to eat healthfully. Nonfat and low-fat alternatives are available for just about any ingredient you can think of. This makes it possible to create a dazzling array of healthy and delicious treats, including nonfat and low-fat versions of many of your favorite foods. In the pages that follow, we'll take a look at low-fat and nonfat cheeses, fat-free spreads and dressings, fat-free egg substitutes, ultra-lean meats, and other ingredients that will insure success in all your fat-free cooking adventures.

Low-Fat and Nonfat Cheeses

Americans have long had a love affair with cheese. For many years, though, people who wanted to reduce the fat in their diet had to also reduce the cheese, or even eliminate cheese entirely. Fortunately, a wide range of nonfat and low-fat products is now available, making it possible to have your cheese and eat it, too. Let's learn about some of the cheeses that you'll be using in your fat-free holiday recipes.

Maximum Daily Fat Intakes

Weight	Recommended Daily Calorie Intake (13--15 calories per pound)	Fat Grams Allowed (20%)	Fat Grams Allowed (25%)
100	1,300--1,500	29--33	36--42
110	1,430--1,650	32--37	40--46
120	1,560--1,800	34--40	43--50
130	1,690--1,950	38--43	47--54
140	1,820--2,100	40--46	51--58
150	1,950--2,250	43--50	54--62
160	2,080--2,400	46--53	58--67
170	2,210--2,550	49--57	61--71
180	2,340--2,700	52--60	65--75
190	2,470--2,850	55--63	69--79
200	2,600--3,000	58--66	72--83

Cottage Cheese. Although often thought of as a diet food, full-fat cottage cheese has 5 grams of fat per 4-ounce serving, making it far from diet fare. Instead, choose nonfat or low-fat cottage cheese, which may be puréed until smooth and used as a base for dips and spreads. Select brands with 1 percent or less milk fat. Most brands of cottage cheese are high in sodium, with about 400 milligrams per half-cup, so it's best to avoid adding salt whenever this cheese is a recipe ingredient. As an alternative, use unsalted cottage cheese, which is available in some stores.

Another option when buying cottage cheese is dry curd cottage cheese. This nonfat version is made without the "dressing" or creaming mixture. Minus the dressing, cottage cheese has a drier consistency; hence its name, "dry curd." Unlike most cottage cheese, dry curd is very low in sodium. Use it as you would nonfat cottage cheese in casseroles, quiches, dips, spreads, salad dressings, and cheesecakes.

Cream Cheese. Regular full-fat cream cheese contains about 10 grams of fat per ounce, making this popular spread a real menace if you're trying to reduce dietary fat. A tasty alternative is light cream cheese, which has only 5 grams of fat per ounce. Still another reduced-fat alternative is Neufchatel cheese, which contains 6 grams of fat per ounce. And, of course, nonfat cream cheese contains no fat at all. Like light cream cheese and Neufchatel, nonfat cream cheese may be used in dips, spreads, and cheesecakes. Look for brands like Philly Free and Healthy Choice.

Firm and Hard Cheeses. Both low-fat and nonfat cheeses of many types----including Swiss, Cheddar, Monterey jack, and mozzarella----are available in most grocery stores. Reduced-fat cheeses generally have 3 to 5 grams of fat per ounce, while nonfat cheeses contain no fat at all. Compare this with whole-milk varieties, which contain 9 to 10 grams of fat per ounce, and you'll realize your savings in fat and calories.

Nonfat and reduced-fat firm and hard cheeses can be used in casseroles, in sauces, and in any other way their full-fat counterparts are used. Look for brands like Alpine Lace Lo, Cracker Barrel Lite, Healthy Choice, Kraft Light Naturals, Kraft Healthy Favorites, Jarlsberg Lite Swiss, and Weight Watchers.

Parmesan Cheese. Full-fat Parmesan cheese typically contains 8 grams of fat per ounce. Fortunately, as is true of most cheeses, reduced-fat and nonfat versions are available. Keep in mind, though, that a little bit of this flavorful cheese goes a long way, so even if you use regular Parmesan in any of the recipes in this book, the total fat per serving will still be quite low.

Pasteurized Processed Cheese Product. Sold in large blocks, this cheese is designed to melt smoothly, and so is intended as a cooking cheese for use in hot cheese dips and similar dishes. When buying nonfat processed cheese products, look for brands like Healthy Choice.

Ricotta Cheese. Ricotta is a mild, slightly sweet, creamy cheese that may be used in dips, spreads, and traditional Italian dishes like lasagna. As the name implies, nonfat ricotta contains no fat at all. Low-fat ricotta and light ricotta, on the other hand, have 1 to 3 grams of fat per ounce, while whole-milk ricotta has 4 grams of fat per ounce.

Soft Curd Farmer Cheese. This soft, spreadable white cheese makes a good low-fat substitute for cream cheese. Brands made with skim milk have about 3 grams of fat per ounce, compared with cream cheese's 10 grams. Soft curd farmer cheese may be used in dips, spreads, and cheesecakes, and as a filling for blintzes. Some brands are made with whole milk, so read the label carefully. Look for a brand like Friendship Farmer Cheese.

Yogurt Cheese. A good substitute for cream cheese in dips, spreads, and cheesecakes, yogurt cheese can be made at home with any brand of plain or flavored yogurt that does not contain gelatin. Simply place the yogurt in a funnel lined with cheesecloth or a coffee filter, and let it drain into a jar in the refrigerator for eight hours or overnight. When the yogurt is reduced by half, it is ready to use. The whey that collects in the jar may be used in place of the liquid in bread and muffin recipes.

Nondairy Cheese Alternatives. If you choose to avoid dairy products because of a lactose intolerance or for another reason, you'll be glad to know that low-fat cheeses made from soymilk, almond milk, and Brazil nut milk are now available in a variety of flavors. Look for brands like Almondrella, Veganrella, and Tofurella.

Measuring Cheese

Throughout the recipes in this book, I have usually expressed the amount of cheese needed in cups. For instance, a recipe may call for 1 cup of cottage cheese or ¼ cup of grated Parmesan. Since you will sometimes buy cheese in chunks and grate it in your own kitchen, or buy packages marked in ounces when the recipe calls for cups, it is useful to understand that the conversion of cheese from ounces (weight) to cups (volume) varies, depending on the texture of the cheese. When using the recipes in *Fat-Free Holiday Recipes,* the following table should help take the guesswork out of these conversions.

Cheese Equivalency Amounts

Cheese	Weight	Equivalent Volume
Cheddar	8 ounces	2 cups shredded or crumbled
Cottage Cheese	8 ounces	1 cup
Cream Cheese	8 ounces	1 cup
Farmer Cheese	8 ounces	1 cup
Mozzarella	8 ounces	2 cups shredded or crumbled
Parmesan	8 ounces	2¼ cups grated
Ricotta	8 ounces	1 cup

Other Low-Fat and Nonfat Dairy Products

Of course, cheese isn't the only dairy product we use in holiday recipes. How about the sour cream in onion dip and the buttermilk in your favorite biscuits? Fortunately, there are low-fat and nonfat versions of these and other dairy products as well.

Buttermilk. Buttermilk adds a rich flavor and texture to baked goods like biscuits, muffins, and cakes, and lends a "cheesy" taste to sauces, cheesecakes, and casseroles. Originally a by-product of butter making, this product should perhaps be called "butterless" milk. Most brands of buttermilk contain from 0.5 to 2 percent fat by weight, but some brands contain as much as 3.5 percent fat. When following the recipes in this book----which call for nonfat buttermilk----choose brands that are no more than 1 percent milk fat.

If you do not have buttermilk on hand, a good substitute can be made by mixing equal parts of nonfat yogurt and skim milk. Alternatively, mix a tablespoon of vinegar or lemon juice with one cup of skim milk, and let it sit for five minutes before using. For a nondairy alternative to buttermilk, mix a tablespoon of vinegar or lemon juice with one cup of soymilk.

Milk. Whole milk, the highest-fat milk available, is 3.5 percent fat by weight and has 8 grams of fat per cup. Instead, choose skim (nonfat) milk, which----with all but a trace of fat removed----has only about 0.5 gram of fat per cup. Another good choice is 1-percent milk, which, as the name implies, is 1 percent fat by weight and contains 2 grams of fat per cup.

Sour Cream. As calorie- and fat-conscious people know, full-fat sour cream can contain almost 500 calories and about 48 grams of fat per cup! Use nonfat sour cream, though, and you'll save 320 calories and 48 grams of fat. Made from cultured nonfat milk thickened with vegetable gums, this product beautifully replaces its fatty counterpart in cold dips, spreads, and sauces. Look for brands like Land O'Lakes Nonfat. Plain nonfat yogurt may also be substituted for sour cream.

Yogurt. Yogurt adds creamy richness and flavor to sauces, baked goods, and casseroles.

And, of course, it is a perfect base for many dips and dressings. In your low-fat cooking, select brands with 1 percent or less milk fat. If you must avoid dairy products, look for soy yogurt, which is available in health foods stores and many grocery stores.

Fat-Free Spreads and Dressings

Like cheeses, spreads and dressings were long a major source of fat and calories. Happily, many low-fat and nonfat alternatives to our high-fat favorites are now available. Let's learn a little more about these fat-saving products.

Margarine. None of the recipes in this book uses margarine or butter of any kind----or oil or shortening, for that matter. But if you are used to spreading foods with margarine, you can easily reduce your dietary fat by switching to a nonfat or reduced-fat margarine, and using it sparingly. Every tablespoon of nonfat margarine that you substitute for regular margarine will save you 11 grams of fat.

Mayonnaise. Nonfat mayonnaise is highly recommended over regular mayonnaise, which is almost pure fat. How can mayonnaise be made without all that oil? Manufacturers use more water and vegetable thickeners. Some commonly available nonfat brands are Kraft Free, Miracle Whip Free, and Smart Beat. Reduced-fat mayonnaise is also available, with half to two-thirds less fat and calories than regular mayonnaise. Look for brands like Hellman's Reduced-Fat, Kraft Light, Blue Plate Light, and Weight Watcher's.

Salad Dressings. Now made in a number of flavors, fat-free dressings contain either no oil or so little oil that they have less than 0.5 grams of fat per tablespoon. Use these dressings instead of oil-based versions to dress your favorite salads or as a delicious basting sauce for grilled foods.

Fat Substitutes for Baking

Almost any moist ingredient can be used to replace the fat in cakes, muffins, quick breads, and other baked goods. The recipes in this book use a variety of fat substitutes. Most of these substitutes, including applesauce, fruit purée, fruit juice, nonfat buttermilk, and mashed pumpkin, are readily available in grocery stores. Two additional substitutes----Prune Butter and Prune Purée----can be easily made at home using the recipes found in Part Four.

Egg Whites and Egg Substitutes

Everyone who cooks knows the value of eggs. Eggs are star ingredients in quiches, add lightness to many casseroles, and are indispensable in a wide range of baked goods. Of course, eggs are also high in cholesterol. For this reason, the recipes in this book call for egg whites or fat-free egg substitute. Just how great are your savings in cholesterol and fat when whole eggs are replaced with one of these ingredients? One large egg contains 80 calories, 5 grams of fat, and 210 milligrams of cholesterol. The equivalent amount of egg white or fat-free egg substitute contains 20 to 30 calories, no fat, and no cholesterol. The benefits of these substitute ingredients are clear.

You may wonder why some of the recipes in this book call for egg whites while others call for egg substitute. In some cases, one ingredient does, in fact, work better than the other. For instance, egg substitute is the best choice when making quiches and puddings. In addition, because they have been pasteurized (heat treated), egg substitutes are safe to use uncooked in eggnogs and salad dressings. On the other hand, when recipes require whipped egg whites, egg substitutes simply do not work.

In most recipes, egg whites and egg substitute can be used interchangeably. Yet, even in these recipes, one may sometimes be listed instead of the other due to ease of measuring. For example, while a cake made with three tablespoons of fat-free egg substitute would turn out just as well if made with three tablespoons of egg whites, this would require you to use *one and a half* large egg whites, making measuring something of a nuisance.

Whenever a recipe calls for egg whites, use *large* egg whites. When selecting an egg substitute, be sure to look for a fat-free brand like Egg Beaters. (Some egg substitutes contain vegetable oil.) When replacing egg whites with egg substitute, or whole eggs with egg whites or egg substitute, use the following guidelines:

1 large egg = 1½ large egg whites
1 large egg = 3 tablespoons egg substitute
1 large egg white = 2 tablespoons egg substitute

Ultra-Lean Poultry, Meat, and Vegetarian Alternatives

Because of the high fat and cholesterol contents of meats, many people have sharply reduced their consumption of meat, have limited themselves to white-meat chicken and turkey, or have totally eliminated meat and poultry from their diet. The good news is that whether you are a sworn meat eater, someone who only occasionally eats meat dishes, or a confirmed vegetarian, plenty of lean meats, lean poultry, and excellent meat substitutes are now available.

The most important point to remember when including poultry and meat in meals is to keep portions to a modest 6 ounces or less per day. For perspective, 3 ounces of meat is the size of a deck of cards. Here are some suggestions for choosing the leanest possible poultry and meat.

Turkey

Although both chicken and turkey have less total fat and saturated fat than beef and pork, your very best bet when buying poultry is turkey. What's the difference between the fat and calorie contents of chicken and turkey? While 3 ounces of chicken breast without skin contain 139 calories and 3 grams of fat, the same amount of turkey breast without skin contains only 119 calories and 1 gram of fat.

Your best defense against fat when preparing and eating poultry is removing the skin and any underlying visible fat. Doing just this eliminates half the fat. If possible, eliminate the skin *before* cooking. Poultry cooked without the skin has been found to have 20 percent less fat than poultry that had the skin removed after cooking. In addition, if you remove the skin after cooking, you will also remove the seasoning.

All of the leanest cuts of turkey come from the turkey breast, so that all have the same amount of fat and calories per serving. Here is what you're likely to find at your local supermarket:

Turkey Cutlets. Turkey cutlets, which are slices of turkey breast, are usually about ¼ inch thick and weigh about 2 to 3 ounces each. These cutlets may be used as a delicious and healthy alternative to boneless chicken breast, pork tenderloin slices, and veal.

Turkey Medallions. Sliced turkey tenderloins, these medallions are usually about 1 inch thick and weigh 2 to 3 ounces each. Substitute them for pork medallions in your favorite recipes.

Turkey Steaks. Cut from the turkey breast, these steaks are about ½ to 1 inch in thickness. Turkey steaks may be baked, broiled, grilled, cut into stir-fry or kabob pieces, or ground for burgers.

Turkey Tenderloins. Large sections of fresh turkey breast, tenderloins usually weigh about 8 ounces each. Tenderloins may be sliced into cutlets, cut into stir-fry or kabob pieces, ground for burgers, or grilled or roasted as is.

Whole Turkey Breast. Perfect for people who love roast turkey but want only the breast meat, turkey breasts weigh 4 to 7 pounds each. These breasts may be roasted with or without stuffing.
Ground Turkey. Ground turkey is the perfect ingredient for use in meatballs, chili, burgers---- in any dish that uses ground meat. When shopping for ground turkey, you'll find that different

products have different percentages of fat. Ground turkey breast, which is only 1 percent fat by weight, is the leanest ground meat you can buy. Ground dark meat turkey made without the skin is 8 to 10 percent fat by weight. Brands with added skin and fat usually contain 15 percent fat. The moral is clear: Always check the labels before making a purchase!

Beef and Pork

Although not as lean as turkey, beef and pork are both considerably leaner today than in decades past. Spurred by competition from the poultry industry, beef and pork producers have changed breeding and feeding practices to reduce the fat content of these products. In addition, butchers are now trimming away more of the fat from retail cuts of meat. The result? On average, grocery store cuts of beef are 27 percent leaner today than they were in the early 1980s, and retail cuts of pork are 43 percent leaner.

Choosing the Best Cuts and Grades. Of course, some cuts of beef and pork are leaner than others. Which are the smartest choices? The table on the next page will guide you in selecting those cuts that are lowest in fat.

While identifying the lowest-fat cuts of meat is an important first step in healthy cooking, be aware that even lean cuts have varying amounts of fat because of differences in *grades.* In general, the higher, and more expensive, grades of meat, like USDA Prime and Choice, have more fat due to a higher degree of *marbling*----internal fat that cannot be trimmed away. USDA Select meats have the least amount of marbling, and therefore the lowest amount of fat. How important are these differences? A USDA Choice piece of meat may have 15 to 20 percent more fat than a USDA Select cut, and USDA Prime may have even more fat. Clearly, the difference is significant. So when choosing beef and pork for your table, by all means check the package for grade. Then look for the least amount of marbling in the cut you

have chosen, and let appearance be the final judge.

Ground Beef. While ground turkey breast is the very best choice when buying ground meat, low-fat ground beef is now available, giving you a second healthy option. One of your best bets is Healthy Choice Ground Beef. A mixture of lean beef and a small amount of oat flour, which is used to hold in moisture, this product is 4 percent fat by weight, giving it about 33 calories and 1 gram of fat per ounce. Other brands of 93- to 96-percent lean ground beef are also on the market. Some use the sea vegetable carrageen instead of oat flour.

Lean Processed Meat

Because of our new fat-consciousness, low-fat sausages, hams, and lunch meats are now available, with just a fraction of the fat of regular processed meats. Many of these low-fat products are used in the recipes in this book.

When a recipe calls for smoked turkey sausage, try a brand like Healthy Choice, which has just 1 gram of fat per ounce. When a recipe calls for ground turkey breakfast sausage, try a brand like Louis Rich. Many stores now make their own fresh turkey sausage, including turkey Italian sausage. When buying these fresh sausages, always check the package and choose the leanest mixture available.

One of the biggest boons to health-conscious party givers are low-fat lunch meats, which allow you to easily prepare a variety of heart-smart hors d'oeuvres and cold cut platters. For recipes that include ham or turkey pastrami, look for Healthy Choice, Butterball, and Oscar Mayer Healthy Favorites----brands with no more than 1 gram of fat per ounce.

Vegetarian Alternatives

Nonmeat alternatives to ground meat can be substituted for ground beef or poultry in any of the recipes in this book. One good choice is Harvest Burger. Made from soybeans, Harvest Burger is rich in protein and has only about 1

Lean Beef and Pork Cuts

Cut (3 ounces, cooked & trimmed)	Calories	
Beef		
Eye of Round	143	4.2 grams
Top Round	153	4.2 grams
Round Tip	157	5.9 grams
Top Sirloin	165	6.1 grams
Pork		
Tenderloin	139	4.1 grams
Ham (95% lean)	112	4.3 grams
Boneless Sirloin Chop	164	5.7 grams
Boneless Loin Roast	165	6.1 grams
Boneless Loin Chops	173	6.6 grams

gram of fat per ounce. Harvest Burger comes packaged as dry nuggets in individual pouches. When rehydrated, the contents of a single pouch is equivalent to one pound of ground meat. Harvest Burger can be shaped into meatballs or patties, and can replace ground meat in dishes like chili.

Texturized vegetable protein (TVP) is yet another alternative to ground meat. Made from defatted soy flour, TVP has about 0.3 grams of fat per ounce. Like Harvest Burger, TVP is packaged as dry nuggets that you rehydrate with water. This product makes an excellent ground meat substitute in chili, tacos, and many other dishes.

Grains and Flours

Just because a food is fat-free does not mean it is good for you. Fat-free products made from refined white flour and refined grains provide few nutrients, and can actually deplete nutrient stores if eaten in excess. Whole grains and whole grain flours, on the other hand, contain a multitude of nutrients such as vitamin E, zinc, magnesium, chromium, potassium, and many other nutrients that are lacking in refined grains. Whole grain products also add fiber to our diets, making our meals more satisfying. You see, fiber----like fat----provides a feeling of fullness. Fiber also helps maintain blood sugar levels, which helps keep hunger at bay.

Fortunately, once accustomed to the heartier taste and texture of whole grains, most people prefer them over tasteless refined grains. Following is a description of some of the whole grain products used in the recipes in this book. Many of these products are readily available in grocery stores, while others may be found in health foods stores and gourmet shops. If you are unable to locate a particular grain or flour in your area, it is probably available by mail order.

Barley. This grain has a nutty light flavor, making it a great substitute for rice in any dish. Barley flour, made from ground barley kernels, is rich in cholesterol-lowering soluble fiber. Slightly sweet in taste, this flour adds a cake-like texture to baked goods, and can be used interchangeably with oat flour in any recipe.

Brown Rice. Brown rice is whole-kernel rice, meaning that all nutrients are intact. With a slightly chewy texture and a pleasant nutty flavor, brown rice makes excellent pilafs and stuffings. *Brown rice flour,* which is simply finely ground brown rice, has a texture similar to cornmeal and adds a mildly sweet flavor to baked goods. Use it in cookies for a crisp and crunchy texture.

Cornmeal. This grain adds a sweet flavor, a lovely golden color, and a crunchy texture to baked goods. Select whole grain (unbolted) cornmeal for the most nutrition. By contrast, bolted cornmeal is nearly whole grain, and de-germed cornmeal is refined.

Oat Bran. Made of the outer part of the oat kernel, oat bran has a sweet, mild flavor and is a concentrated source of cholesterol-lowering soluble fiber. Oat bran helps retain moisture in baked goods, making it a natural for fat-free baking. Look for it in the hot cereal section of your grocery store, and choose the softer, more finely ground products, like Quaker Oat Bran. Coarsely ground oat bran makes excellent hot cereal, but is not the best for baking.

Oats. Loaded with cholesterol-lowering soluble fiber, oats add a chewy texture and sweet flavor to a variety of dishes. *Oat flour* is widely available in health foods stores and many grocery stores, and can also be made at home by grinding quick-cooking rolled oats in a blender. (Look for oats that cook in one minute.) Like oat bran, this flour retains moisture in baked goods, reducing the need for fat.

Unbleached Flour. This is refined white flour that has not been subjected to a bleaching process. Unbleached white flour lacks significant amounts of nutrients compared with whole wheat flour, but does contain more vitamin E than bleached flour.

Whole Grain Wheat. Available in many forms, this grain is perhaps easiest to use in the form of *bulgur wheat.* Cracked wheat that is precooked and dried, bulgur wheat can be prepared in a matter of minutes, and can be used to replace rice in any recipe.

Whole wheat flour, made of ground whole grain wheat kernels, includes the grain's nutrient-rich bran and germ. Nutritionally speaking, whole wheat flour is far superior to refined flour. Sadly, many people grew up eating refined baked goods, and find whole grain products too heavy for their taste. A good way to learn to enjoy whole grain flours is to use part whole wheat and part unbleached flour in recipes, and gradually increase the amount of whole wheat used over time. (1 cup plus 1 tablespoon unbleached flour can replace 1 cup of whole wheat flour in recipes.)

When muffin, quick bread, cake, and cookie recipes call for whole wheat flour, *whole wheat pastry flour* works best, although regular whole wheat flour may be used with good results. Whole wheat pastry flour produces lighter, softer-textured baked goods than regular whole wheat flour because it is made from a softer (lower-protein) wheat and is more finely

ground. Look for whole wheat pastry flour in health foods stores and many grocery stores.

White whole wheat flour is another excellent option for baking. Made from hard white wheat instead of the hard red wheat used to make regular whole wheat flour, white whole wheat flour is sweeter and lighter tasting than its red-wheat counterpart. To substitute white whole wheat flour for other flours, use the following guidelines:

1 cup white whole wheat flour = 1 cup unbleached (refined) flour
1 cup + 1 tablespoon white whole wheat flour 1 cup whole wheat pastry flour
1 cup + 1 tablespoon white whole wheat flour 1 cup regular whole wheat flour

Sweeteners

Refined white sugar contains almost no nutrients. In fact, when eaten in excess, refined sugar can actually deplete body stores of essential nutrients like chromium and the B vitamins. Of course, a moderate amount of sugar is usually not a problem for people who eat an otherwise healthy diet. What's moderate? No more than 10 percent of your daily intake of calories should come from sugar. For an individual who needs 2,000 calories a day to maintain his or her weight, this amounts to an upper limit of 12.5 teaspoons (about ¼ cup) of sugar a day. Naturally, a diet that is lower in sugar is even better.

The baked-goods and dessert recipes in this book contain 25 to 50 percent less sugar than traditional recipes do. Ingredients like fruit juices, fruit purées, and dried fruits; flavorings and spices like vanilla extract, nutmeg, and cinnamon; and mildly sweet flours like oat and barley have often been used to reduce the need for sugar.

The recipes in this book call for moderate amounts of white sugar, brown sugar, and different liquid sweeteners. However, a large number of sweeteners are now available, and you should feel free to substitute one sweetener for another, using your own tastes, your desire for high-nutrient ingredients, and your pocketbook as a guide. (Some of the newer less-refined sweeteners are far more expensive than traditional sweeteners.) For best results, replace granular sweeteners with other granular sweeteners, and substitute liquid sweeteners for other liquid sweeteners. You can, of course, replace a liquid with granules, or vice versa, but adjustments in other recipe ingredients will have to be made. (For each cup of liquid sweetener substituted for granular sweetener, reduce the liquid by ¼ to ⅓ cup.) Also be aware that each sweetener has its own unique flavor and its own degree of sweetness, making some sweeteners better suited to particular recipes.

Following is a description of some of the sweeteners commonly available in grocery stores, health foods stores, and gourmet shops. Those sweeteners that can't be found in local stores can usually be ordered by mail.

Apple Butter. Sweet and thick, apple butter is made by cooking down apples with apple juice and spices. Many brands also contain added sugar, but some are sweetened only with juice. Use apple butter as you would honey to sweeten products in which a little spice will enhance the flavor. Spice cakes, bran muffins, and oatmeal cookies are all delicious made with apple butter.

Brown Rice Syrup. Commonly available in health foods stores, brown rice syrup is made by converting the starch in brown rice into sugar. This syrup is mildly sweet----about 30 to 60 percent as sweet as sugar, depending on the brand----and has a delicate malt flavor. Perhaps most important, brown rice syrup retains most of the nutrients found in the rice from which it was made. This sweetener is a good substitute for honey or other liquid sweeteners whenever you want to tone down the sweetness of a recipe.

Brown Sugar. This granulated sweetener is simply refined white sugar that has been coated with a thin film of molasses. Light brown sugar is lighter in color than regular brown sugar, but not lower in calories as the name might imply. Because this sweetener contains some molasses, brown sugar has more calcium, iron, and potassium than white sugar. But like most sugars, brown sugar is no nutritional powerhouse. The advantage to using this sweetener is that it is more flavorful than white sugar so that less can generally be used.

Date Sugar. Made from ground dried dates, date sugar provides copper, magnesium, iron, and B vitamins. With a distinct date flavor, date sugar is delicious in breads, cakes, and muffins. Because it does not dissolve as readily as white sugar does, it's best to mix date sugar with the recipe's liquid ingredients and let it sit for a few minutes before proceeding with the recipe. Because date sugar is less dense than white sugar, it is only about two-thirds as sweet. However, date sugar is more flavorful, and so can often be substituted for white sugar on a cup-for-cup basis.

Fruit Juice Concentrates. Frozen juice concentrates add sweetness and flavor to baked goods while enhancing nutritional value. Use the concentrates as you would honey or other liquid sweeteners, but beware----too much will be overpowering. Always keep cans of frozen orange and apple juice concentrate in the freezer just for baking. Pineapple and tropical fruit blends also make good sweeteners, and white grape juice is ideal when you want a more neutral flavor.

Fruit Source. Made from white grape juice and brown rice, this sweetener has a rather neutral flavor and is about as sweet as white sugar.

Fruit Source is available in both granular and liquid forms. Use the liquid as you would honey, and the granules as you would sugar. The granules do not dissolve as readily as sugar does, so mix Fruit Source with the recipe's liquid ingredients and let it sit for a few minutes before proceeding with the recipe.

Fruit Spreads, Jams, and Preserves. Available in a variety of flavors, these products make delicious sweeteners. For best flavor and nutrition, choose a brand made from fruits and fruit juice concentrate, with little or no added sugar, and select a flavor that is compatible with the baked goods you're making. Use as you would any liquid sweetener.

Honey. Contrary to popular belief, honey is not significantly more nutritious than sugar, but it does add a nice flavor to baked goods. It also adds moistness, reducing the need for fat. The sweetest of the liquid sweeteners, honey is generally 20 to 30 percent sweeter than sugar. Be sure to consider this when making substitutions.

Maple Sugar. Made from dehydrated maple syrup, granulated maple sugar adds a distinct maple flavor to baked goods. Powdered maple sugar is also available, and can be used to replace powdered white sugar in glazes.

Maple Syrup. The boiled-down sap of sugar maple trees, maple syrup adds delicious flavor to all baked goods, and also provides some potassium and other nutrients. Use it as you would honey or molasses.

Molasses. Light, or Barbados, molasses is pure sugarcane juice boiled down into a thick syrup. Light molasses provides some calcium, potassium, and iron, and is delicious in spice cakes, muffins, breads, and cookies. Blackstrap molasses is a by-product of the sugar-refining process. Very rich in calcium, potassium, and iron, it has a slightly bitter, strong flavor, and is half as sweet as refined sugar. Because of its distinctive taste, more than a few tablespoons in a recipe is overwhelming.

Sucanat. Granules of evaporated sugarcane juice, Sucanat tastes similar to brown sugar. This sweetener provides small amounts of potassium, chromium, calcium, iron, and vitamins A and C. Use it as you would any other granulated sugar.

Sugarcane Syrup. The process used to make sugarcane syrup is similar to that of making light molasses. Consequently, the syrup has a molasses-like flavor and is nutritionally comparable to the other sweetener.

Throughout our discussion of sweeteners, we have mentioned that some sweeteners are higher in nutrients than others. Just how much variation is there among sweeteners? The table on the next page compares the amounts of selected nutrients found in one-quarter cup of different sweeteners. Pay special attention to how the sweeteners compare with white sugar, the most refined of all the sweeteners.

Other Ingredients

Aside from the ingredients already discussed, a few more items may prove useful as you venture into fat-free cooking. Some ingredients may already be familiar to you, while others may become new additions to your pantry.

Dried Cranberries. These tasty treats----which are simply cranberries that have been sweetened and dried----look like red raisins, and are sometimes referred to as "craisins." Dried cranberries add a festive touch to muffins, cookies, and other baked goods, and provide a nice change of pace from raisins. Look for them in specialty stores, health foods stores, and many grocery stores. If you cannot find dried cranberries, golden raisins are a good substitute.

Other Dried Fruits. A wide variety of dried fruits are available. Dried pineapple, apricots, prunes, dates, and peaches are available in most grocery stores, while health foods and other specialty stores often carry dried mangoes, papaya, cherries, and blueberries. These

Comparing Sweeteners

Sweetener (1/4 cup)	Calories	Calcium (mg)	Iron (mg)	Potassium (mg)
Apple Butter	130	10	0.5	176
Brown Rice Syrup	256	3	0.1	140
Brown Sugar	205	47	1.2	189
Date Sugar	88	10	0.4	209
Fruit Juice Concentrate (apple)	116	14	0.6	315
Fruit Juice Concentrate (orange)	113	23	0.3	479
Fruit Preserves	216	8	0	12
Fruit Source (granules)	192	16	0.4	142
Fruit Source (syrup)	176	15	0.4	138
Honey	240	0	0.5	27
Maple Sugar	176	45	0.8	137
Maple Syrup	202	83	1.0	141
Molasses, Blackstrap	170	548	20.2	2,342
Molasses, Light	172	132	4.3	732
Sucanat	144	41	1.6	162
Sugar Cane Syrup	210	48	2.9	340
White Sugar	192	1	0	2

fruits add interest to muffins, cookies, and other baked goods, and often reduce the need for sugar. If you cannot find the type of dried fruit called for in a recipe, feel free to substitute another type.

Toasted Wheat Germ. This ingredient adds crunch and a nutty flavor to baked goods. A supernutritious food, with only half the fat of nuts, wheat germ provides significant amounts of vitamin E and minerals.

A Word About Salt

Salt, a combination of sodium and chloride, enhances the flavors of many foods. However, most health experts recommend a maximum of 2,400 milligrams per day, the equivalent of about one teaspoon of salt. For this reason, salt is not often used in the recipes in this book. A minimal use of salt-laden processed ingredients, as well as the wise use of herbs and spices, keeps the salt content under control without compromising taste.

ABOUT THE NUTRITIONAL ANALYSIS

The Food Processor II (ESHA Research) computer nutrition analysis system, along with product information from manufacturers, was used to calculate the nutritional information for all the recipes in this book. Nutrients are always listed per one piece, one muffin, one slice of bread, one cookie, one serving, etc.

Sometimes, recipes give you options regarding the ingredients. For instance, you might be able to choose between nonfat cream cheese and reduced-fat cream cheese, nonfat mayonnaise and reduced-fat mayonnaise, or raisins and nuts. This will help you create dishes that suit your tastes. Just keep in mind that the nutritional analysis is based on the first ingredient listed.

In your quest for fat-free eating, you might be inclined to choose fat-free cheese over reduced-fat cheese, and to omit any optional nuts. Be aware, though, that if you are not used to nonfat cheeses, it might be wise to start by using reduced-fat products. Should you opt to omit the nuts? Not necessarily. Nuts are high in fat, but they also contain essential minerals and vitamin E. Some studies have even indicated that people who eat nuts as part of a healthy diet have less heart disease. If you like nuts, feel free to use them in recipes. In fat-free recipes like the ones in this book, you can afford to add a few nuts or to choose the higher-fat ingredient.

WHERE DOES THE FAT COME FROM IN FAT-FREE RECIPES?

You may notice that even though a recipe may contain no oil, butter, cheese, margarine, shortening, nuts, chocolate chips, or other fatty ingredients, it still contains a small amount of fat (less than one gram). This is because many natural ingredients contain some fat. Whole grains, for example, store a small amount of oil in their germ, the center portion of the grain. This oil is very beneficial because it is loaded with vitamin E, an antioxidant. The germ also provides an abundance of other vitamins and minerals. Products made from refined grains and refined flours----ingredients that have been stripped of the germ----do have slightly less fat than whole grain versions, but they also have far less nutrients.

Other ingredients, too, naturally contain small amounts of fat. For instance, fruits and vegetables, like grains, contain some oil. And, again, the oil also provides many important nutrients. Olives, nuts, and lean meats also contribute fat to some recipes. However, when used in small quantities, the amount of fat is insignificant. In fact, the majority of recipes in this book contain less than 0.5 grams of fat per serving. This qualifies them for the FDA designation *fat-free*.

This book is filled with recipes that make entertaining elegant, simple, and satisfying. Whether you are having a few people over for coffee and dessert, a casual dinner party, or an open house, you will find something to meet your needs. So eat well and enjoy! The dishes you are about to make will not only be delicious, but will also be foods that you can feel good about serving to your friends and family.

Part One

Hors D'Oeuvres for All Seasons

Whether you are planning to have a few people over for light hors d'oeuvres or an open house for fifty, this collection of recipes is sure to meet your needs with a wealth of ideas for fat-free and low-fat finger foods and snacks that are so delicious, no one will even guess that they're good for you. A few simple ingredient substitutions make a big fat difference in traditional party favorites. Ultra-lean ground meats, reduced-fat and nonfat cheeses, nonfat sour cream, and nonfat mayonnaise star in meatballs, dips, spreads, and finger sandwiches that are every bit as tempting as their traditional counterparts.

The following pages first present recipes for hot treats----meatballs, kabobs, hot dips, and other savory snacks that can be passed around on platters or kept warm in a chafing dish for fuss-free serving. This is followed by a tempting variety of finger sandwiches and other cold pick-up snacks, as well as a wide range of recipes for perhaps the most popular and versatile party foods of all----cold dips and spreads round out the selection, guaranteeing that your next party will be a memorable one.

HOT STUFF

Spicy Barbecue Meatballs

Yield: 60 appetizers

MEATBALLS

1½ pounds ground turkey breast
   or 96% lean ground beef

¾ cup quick-cooking oats

2 egg whites

1 cup finely chopped onion

1½ teaspoons crushed fresh garlic

¼ cup minced fresh parsley

1 teaspoon dried oregano

1½ teaspoons beef bouillon granules

½ teaspoon ground black pepper

SAUCE

1 can (8 ounces) unsalted tomato
   sauce

3 tablespoons honey

3 tablespoons spicy mustard

1¼ teaspoons chili powder

½ teaspoon Tabasco pepper sauce

1. Combine the meatball ingredients in a medium-sized bowl, and mix thoroughly. Coat a baking sheet with nonstick cooking spray. Shape the meatball mixture into 60 (1-inch) balls, and place the meatballs on the baking sheet.

2. Bake the meatballs at 350°F for about 25 minutes, or until thoroughly cooked. Transfer the meatballs to a chafing dish or Crock-Pot heated casserole to keep warm.

3. Combine the sauce ingredients in a small saucepan, and simmer over medium-low heat just until hot. Pour the sauce over the meatballs, toss gently to mix, and serve.

NUTRITIONAL FACTS (PER APPETIZER)

Calories: 24	Fat: 0.2 g	Protein: 3.3 g
Cholesterol: 7 mg	Fiber: 0.2 g	Sodium: 35 mg

Bacon-Wrapped Shrimp

1. Cut each piece of bacon in half lengthwise. Then cut each slice crosswise to make 20 pieces. Wrap 1 piece of bacon around each shrimp, and secure with a wooden toothpick.

2. Place the shrimp on a baking sheet, and bake at 350°F for about 20 minutes, or until the shrimp turn pink. Transfer to a serving platter, and serve hot.

Yield: 20 appetizers

5 slices turkey bacon

20 large raw shrimp (about 8 ounces), peeled and deveined

NUTRITIONAL FACTS (PER APPETIZER)

Calories: 22	Fat: 0.6 g	Protein: 3.4 g
Cholesterol: 30 mg	Fiber: 0 g	Sodium: 89 mg

Variation

For a different taste----and more crunch----substitute whole water chestnuts for the shrimp.

Florentine Stuffed Mushrooms

If you can't find extra-large mushrooms in your grocery store, use 32 medium-sized mushrooms, and place 1½ teaspoons of stuffing in each cap.

1. Remove and discard the mushroom stems. Wash the mushroom caps and pat dry. Set aside.

2. Place the spinach, thyme or oregano, and garlic in a large nonstick skillet. Sauté over medium heat just until the spinach is wilted. (Add a tablespoon of white wine or broth if the skillet is too dry.)

3. Remove the skillet from the heat and allow the spinach to cool slightly. Stir in the scallions, Parmesan cheese, and sour

Yield: 16 appetizers

16 extra-large stuffing mushrooms

3 cups (packed) chopped raw spinach

½ teaspoon dried thyme or oregano

½ teaspoon crushed fresh garlic

2 scallions, finely chopped

¼ cup grated nonfat Parmesan cheese

¼ cup nonfat sour cream

3 cups soft bread crumbs

2 tablespoons white wine or broth

Lemon wedges (garnish)

cream. Add the bread crumbs and toss gently, just until the crumbs are moistened.

4. Place a heaping teaspoonful of stuffing in each mushroom cap. Place 2 tablespoons of white wine or broth in a shallow baking pan, and arrange the mushrooms in the pan.

5. Bake at 400°F for 20 minutes, or until lightly browned on top. Transfer the mushrooms to a serving platter, garnish with the lemon wedges, and serve hot.

NUTRITIONAL FACTS (PER APPETIZER)

Calories: 40	Fat: 0.4 g	Protein: 2.6 g
Cholesterol: 0 mg	Fiber: 1.5 g	Sodium: 80 mg

Teriyaki Turkey Kabobs

Yield: 32 appetizers

2 pounds boneless skinless turkey breasts

1 can (20 ounces) unsweetened pineapple chunks, undrained

2 tablespoons reduced-sodium soy sauce

2 tablespoons brown sugar

1½ teaspoons freshly grated ginger root, or ½ teaspoon ground ginger

1 teaspoon crushed fresh garlic

32 whole water chestnuts

1. Cut the turkey into 32 chunks, 1 inch each. Set aside.

2. Drain the pineapple chunks. Reserve the juice for immediate use, and wrap and refrigerate the pineapple. Combine the juice, soy sauce, brown sugar, ginger, and garlic in a shallow dish. Place the turkey in this marinade, cover, and refrigerate for several hours or overnight.

3. Create individual kabobs by skewering 1 piece of pineapple, 1 turkey chunk, and 1 water chestnut on each of 32 wooden toothpicks. Place the skewers in a shallow baking pan, and pour ¼ cup of the marinade over the kabobs.

4. Bake at 350°F for about 20 minutes, or until the turkey is fork-tender and no longer pink inside. Drain off any excess liquid, transfer to a serving platter, and serve hot.

NUTRITIONAL FACTS (PER APPETIZER)

Calories: 44	Fat: 0.3 g	Protein: 7 g
Cholesterol: 19 mg	Fiber: 0.3 g	Sodium: 30 mg

Hot Artichoke Appetizers

1. If the artichoke hearts are large, cut them in quarters. If they are small, cut them in half. You should have about 40 pieces.

2. Combine the marinade ingredients in a blender, and process for 30 seconds, or until smooth. Place the artichoke hearts in a shallow dish, and pour the marinade over them. Cover and refrigerate for several hours or overnight.

3. Cut each ham slice into eight ½-inch strips. Drain the artichoke hearts, and discard the marinade. Wrap a ham strip around each artichoke piece, and secure with a wooden toothpick.

4. Place the wrapped artichokes in a shallow baking dish, and bake at 350°F for 10 to 15 minutes, or until thoroughly heated. Transfer to a serving platter, and serve hot.

Yield: 40 appetizers

3 packages (10 ounces each) frozen artichoke hearts, thawed, or 3 cans (14 ounces each) artichoke hearts, drained

5 4-inch square slices (1 ounce each) lean ham

MARINADE

⅓ cup Dijon mustard

⅓ cup water

¼ cup finely chopped onion

1 tablespoon sugar

NUTRITIONAL FACTS (PER APPETIZER)

Calories: 11	Fat: 0.3 g	Protein: 1.1 g
Cholesterol: 2 mg	Fiber: 1 g	Sodium: 49 mg

Sensational Broccoli Strudels

1. Combine the broccoli, mozzarella cheese, egg substitute, and mustard in a medium-sized bowl, and stir to mix well. Set aside.

2. Spread the phyllo dough out on a clean dry surface. You should have a 14-x-18-inch sheet that is 12 layers thick. Cover the phyllo dough with plastic wrap to prevent it from drying out as you work. (Remove sheets as you need them, being sure to re-cover the remaining dough.)

3. Remove 1 sheet of phyllo dough, and lay it flat on a clean dry surface with the short end near you. Spray the strip lightly with cooking spray. Top with another phyllo

Yield: 28 appetizers

1 package (10 ounces) frozen chopped broccoli, thawed and squeezed dry

1 cup shredded nonfat or reduced-fat mozzarella cheese

¼ cup fat-free egg substitute, or 2 egg whites

1 tablespoon Dijon mustard

12 sheets phyllo dough

Nonstick cooking spray

sheet, and spray lightly with cooking spray. Repeat with a third sheet.

4. Spread ¼ of the filling over the lower third of the stacked sheets, leaving a 4-inch margin on each side. Fold the left and right edges inward to enclose the filling, and roll the sheet up from the bottom, jelly-roll style. Repeat with the remaining dough and filling to make 4 rolls.

5. Coat a baking sheet with nonstick cooking spray. Place the rolls seam side down on the sheet, and spray the tops lightly with cooking spray. Bake at 350°F for 25 minutes, or until light golden brown.

6. Remove the rolls from the oven, and allow to cool for 5 minutes. Slice each cooled roll into 7 (¾-inch) slices, transfer to a serving platter, and serve warm.

Time-Saving Tip

Several days before the party, prepare the strudels to the point of baking, and freeze them in freezer bags or airtight containers. Arrange the strudels on a coated baking sheet and allow them to sit at room temperature for 45 minutes before baking.

Making Sensational Broccoli Strudels.

NUTRITIONAL FACTS (PER APPETIZER)

| Calories: 39 | Fat: 0.4 g | Protein: 2.8 g |
| Cholesterol: 0 mg | Fiber: 0.4 g | Sodium: 75 mg |

a. Spread the filling over the dough.

b. Fold the left and right edges inward over the filling.

c. Roll the folded sheet up.

Flaky Spinach Pies

1. Combine the spinach, ricotta, mozzarella, Parmesan, and oregano in a medium-sized bowl, and stir to mix well. Set aside.

2. Spread the phyllo dough out on a clean dry surface. You should have a 14-x-18-inch sheet that is 20 layers thick. Cut the phyllo dough lengthwise into 4 long strips. Cover the phyllo dough with plastic wrap to prevent it from drying out as you work. (Remove strips as you need them, being sure to re-cover the remaining dough.)

3.
Remove 1 strip of phyllo dough, and lay it flat on a clean dry surface. Spray the strip lightly with cooking spray. Top with another phyllo strip, and spray lightly with cooking spray. Spread 2 teaspoons of filling over the bottom right-hand corner of the double phyllo strip. Fold the filled corner up and over to the left, so that the corner meets the left side of the strip. Continue folding in this manner until you form a triangle of dough. Repeat with the remaining dough and filling to make 40 triangles.

4. Coat a baking sheet with nonstick cooking spray. Place the appetizers seam side down on the sheet, and bake at 375°F for 15 to 20 minutes, or until nicely browned. Transfer to a serving platter, and serve hot.

Time-Saving Tip

To speed last-minute party preparations, prepare the pies in advance to the point of baking, and arrange them in single layers in airtight plastic containers, separating the layers with sheets of waxed paper. Freeze until the day of the party. Then arrange the frozen pies on a coated baking sheet, and allow them to sit at room temperature for 45 minutes before baking.

NUTRITIONAL FACTS (PER APPETIZER)

Calories: 43	Fat: 0.3 g	Protein: 2.8 g
Cholesterol: 0 mg	Fiber: 0.4 g	Sodium: 69 mg

Yield: 40 appetizers

1 package (10 ounces) frozen chopped spinach, thawed and squeezed dry

1 cup nonfat ricotta cheese

½ cup shredded nonfat or reduced-fat mozzarella cheese

¼ cup grated nonfat or reduced-fat Parmesan cheese

½ teaspoon dried oregano

20 sheets phyllo dough (1 pound)

Olive oil cooking spray

Making Flaky Spinach Pies.

a. Cut the dough into 4 strips.

b. Fold the filled corner up and over.

c. Continue folding to form a triangle.

Shrimp Wrapped in Snow Peas

Yield: 64 appetizers

64 large snow peas (about ½ pound)

64 large shrimp (about 1¾ pounds), peeled and cooked

DIPPING SAUCE

3 tablespoons honey

¼ cup Dijon mustard

¾ cup plain nonfat yogurt

1. Combine the sauce ingredients in a small bowl, and stir to mix well. Set aside.

2. Place the snow peas in a microwave or stove-top steamer. Cover and cook on high power or over medium-high heat for 3 minutes, or just until the snow peas are bright green and pliable. Rinse with cool water, and set aside.

3. Wrap a snow pea around each shrimp, and secure with a toothpick. Arrange on a serving platter and serve with the Dipping Sauce.

NUTRITIONAL FACTS
(PER APPETIZER WITH ½ TEASPOON SAUCE)

Calories: 21	Fat: 0.2 g	Protein: 3.4 g
Cholesterol: 27 mg	Fiber: 0.2 g	Sodium: 41 mg

Veggie-Cheese Finger Sandwiches

Yield: 32 appetizers

2 cups nonfat or reduced-fat cream cheese, softened to room temperature

¼ cup finely chopped onion

¼ cup finely chopped green bell pepper

¼ cup grated carrot

2 tablespoons finely chopped fresh parsley

1–2 teaspoons prepared horseradish or spicy mustard

16 slices firm whole wheat, rye, or pumpernickel bread

1. Place the softened cream cheese in a medium-sized bowl. Combine the vegetables, parsley, and horseradish or mustard in a small bowl. Stir the vegetable mixture into the softened cream cheese. Cover and chill for several hours to allow the flavors to blend.

2. Place ¼ cup of filling on each of 8 slices of bread. Top each slice with one of the remaining slices, making 8 sandwiches. Trim the crusts from the bread, and cut each sandwich into 4 fingers. Arrange the sandwiches on a platter and serve.

NUTRITIONAL FACTS (PER APPETIZER)

Calories: 51	Fat: 0.4 g	Protein: 4.5 g
Cholesterol: 2 mg	Fiber: 1.1 g	Sodium: 169 mg

COLD STUFF

High Rollers

Simple to make and festive in appearance, these appetizers go fast, so be sure to make plenty.

1. Spread each tortilla with 3 tablespoons of cream cheese, extending the cheese to the outer edges. Lay 2 ounces of sliced turkey over the *bottom half only* of each tortilla, leaving a 1-inch margin on each outer edge. Place 1 ounce of sliced Swiss cheese over the turkey, and spread with 1 tablespoon of ranch dressing. Arrange 6 spinach leaves over the Swiss, and sprinkle with 1 tablespoon of olives if desired. Arrange 6 red bell pepper or tomato slices over the olive layer. Top with ¼ cup of artichoke hearts.

2. Starting at the bottom, roll each tortilla up tightly. Cut a 1¼-inch piece off each end and discard. Slice the remaining tortillas into six 1¼-inch pieces. Arrange the rolls on a platter and serve.

Yield: 48 appetizers

8 flour tortillas (10-inch rounds)

1½ cups nonfat or reduced-fat cream cheese (plain or garlic-and-herb flavor)

1 pound thinly sliced turkey breast

8 ounces thinly sliced nonfat or reduced-fat Swiss cheese

½ cup fat-free ranch dressing

48 fresh tender spinach leaves

½ cup finely chopped black olives (optional)

48 very thin slices of red bell pepper or tomato

1 can (14 ounces) artichoke hearts, drained and chopped

NUTRITIONAL FACTS (PER APPETIZER)

Calories: 55	Fat: 0.8 g	Protein: 6 g
Cholesterol: 6 mg	Fiber: 0.7 g	Sodium: 122 mg

Time-Saving Tip

To avoid a last-minute rush, make High Rollers the day before your party, cover the hors d'oeuvres with plastic wrap, and refrigerate. The next day, simply remove the plastic wrap and serve.

Salmon Mousse

Yield: 4 cups

½ cup water or unsalted chicken broth

1 envelope unflavored gelatin

2 cans (6 ounces each) boneless skinless pink salmon

1½ cups nonfat sour cream

½ cup finely chopped celery

¼ cup finely chopped onion

2–3 tablespoons minced fresh dill, or 2–3 teaspoons dried

1 tablespoon lemon juice

For variety, substitute flaked crab meat for the salmon.

1. Place the water or broth in a small saucepan, and sprinkle the gelatin over the top. Set aside for 5 minutes. Then place over low heat and cook, stirring constantly, just until the gelatin is dissolved. Let cool to room temperature.

2. Drain the salmon, place it in a medium-sized bowl, and separate the meat into fine flakes. Add the cooled gelatin mixture and the remaining ingredients, and stir to mix well. Pour the mixture into an ungreased 4-cup fish-shaped mold, cover, and chill for several hours or overnight.

3. To unmold the mousse, dip the mold in warm----but not hot----water to the depth of the gelatin mixture for 5 to 10 seconds. Remove the mold from the water, and loosen the edges with a sharp knife. Invert the mold onto a serving platter, surround with whole grain crackers and fresh vegetables, and serve cold.

NUTRITIONAL FACTS (PER TABLESPOON)

Calories: 13	Fat: 0.3 g	Protein: 1.3 g
Cholesterol: 2 mg	Fiber: 0 g	Sodium: 26 mg

Creamy Cucumber Dip

Yield: 2¼ cups

1 medium cucumber, peeled, seeded, and cut in chunks

2 scallions, finely chopped

¼ teaspoon ground white pepper

2 cups nonfat sour cream

1. Place the cucumber in a food processor or blender, and process until finely chopped. Roll the chopped cucumber in a kitchen towel, and squeeze out any excess moisture.

2. Place the sour cream in a medium-sized bowl, and fold in the cucumber and the remaining ingredients. Transfer the dip to a serving dish, cover, and chill for several hours.

3. Serve with raw vegetables and whole grain crackers.

NUTRITIONAL FACTS (PER TABLESPOON)

Calories: 12	Fat: 0 g	Protein: 0.8 g
Cholesterol: 0 mg	Fiber: 0 g	Sodium: 16 mg

Chutney Dip

1. Combine the ingredients in a medium-sized bowl. Transfer the dip to a serving dish, cover, and chill for several hours.

2. Serve with pita bread wedges, whole wheat crackers, celery sticks, apple wedges, and thinly sliced turkey breast.

Yield: 2⅓ cups

2 cups nonfat sour cream or yogurt cheese (page 6)

⅓ cup mango chutney

1 teaspoon curry powder (optional)

NUTRITIONAL FACTS (PER TABLESPOON)

Calories: 16	Fat: 0 g	Protein: 0.8 g
Cholesterol: 0 mg	Fiber: 0 g	Sodium: 29 mg

Broccoli Cheese Dip

1. Combine the sour cream and mayonnaise in a medium-sized bowl, and stir to mix well. Fold in the broccoli and cheese. Transfer the dip to a serving dish, cover, and chill for at least 1 hour.

2. Serve with sliced bagels or vegetable crackers.

Yield: 4 cups

2 cups nonfat sour cream

½ cup nonfat or reduced-fat mayonnaise

1 package (10 ounces) frozen chopped broccoli, thawed and squeezed dry

1 cup shredded nonfat or reduced-fat Cheddar cheese

NUTRITIONAL FACTS (PER TABLESPOON)

Calories: 12	Fat: 0 g	Protein: 1.2 g
Cholesterol: 0 mg	Fiber: 0.1 g	Sodium: 39 mg

Savannah Seafood Spread

Yield: 12 servings

1 block (8 ounces) nonfat or reduced-fat cream cheese

¾ cup (4–5 ounces) frozen cooked whole salad shrimp, thawed, or ¾ cup diced cooked shrimp

¾ cup flaked cooked crab meat

SAUCE

¾ cup no-added-salt or low-sodium ketchup

2 tablespoons prepared horseradish

2 tablespoons lemon juice

1. Place the block of cheese in the center of a serving plate. Combine the shrimp and crab meat in a medium-sized bowl, and pile over the cheese. Combine the sauce ingredients in a small bowl, and pour over the seafood.

2. Serve with whole scallions, celery sticks, and whole grain crackers.

NUTRITIONAL FACTS (PER SERVING)

| Calories: 57 | Fat: 0.3 g | Protein: 8.2 g |
| Cholesterol: 32 mg | Fiber: 0.4 g | Sodium: 150 mg |

Super Stuffed Veggies

It takes a matter of minutes to turn fresh vegetables and any of the dips or sandwich fillings presented in this book into delicious stuffed veggies. Serve these veggies as healthy hors d'oeuvres, or use them to decorate platters of finger sandwiches and canapés. The following ideas should get you started, but do experiment with other vegetables and dips to find the combinations that you like best.

☐ Slice off the tops of cherry tomatoes, scoop out the seeds, and fill with Creamy Cucumber Dip (page 26).

☐ Cut peeled cucumbers into ¾- to 1-inch-thick slices. Scoop out some of the seeds, creating a cucumber cup with a ¼-inch-thick shell. Fill with Savannah Seafood Spread (page 28).

☐ Cut celery into 2- or 3-inch lengths, and fill with Garlic and Sun Dried Tomato spread (page 29).

☐ Boil new potatoes until tender but firm. Cut a thin slice off the bottom of each potato so that it will sit upright, and scoop out some of the flesh, leaving a ½-inch shell. Fill with Broccoli Cheese Dip (page 27).

Garlic and Sun-Dried Tomato Spread

Yield: 2 cups

1. Place the beans in a large pot, add 4 cups of water, and soak for at least 4 hours. Drain off the water, and add 2 cups of fresh water and the whole garlic cloves. Cover and simmer over low heat for 1½ hours, or until the beans are very tender and all of the liquid has been absorbed. (Periodically check the pot during cooking, and add more water if needed.)

2. Add the tomatoes and water to pot. Cover and simmer for 5 minutes. Cool slightly, and place in a food processor with the remaining ingredients. Process until smooth.

3. Transfer the spread to a serving dish, and serve at room temperature with French bread or toasted wedges of pita bread.

1 cup dried navy beans or Great Northern beans, sorted

1 head garlic, separated into cloves and peeled

½ cup chopped sun-dried tomatoes (not packed in oil)

½ cup water

1 tablespoon olive oil (optional)

¼ teaspoon salt

⅛ teaspoon ground white pepper

NUTRITIONAL FACTS (PER TABLESPOON)

Calories: 22	Fat: 0 g	Protein: 1.3 g
Cholesterol: 0 mg	Fiber: 1.3 g	Sodium: 20 mg

Lentil Paté

Yield: 2 cups

1. Place all the ingredients in a medium-sized pot, and bring the mixture to a boil over high heat. Reduce the heat to low, cover, and simmer for 25 to 30 minutes, or until the lentils are very soft and all of the liquid has been absorbed. (Periodically check the pot during cooking, and add more water if needed.)

2. Cool the mixture slightly, and place in a food processor or blender. Process until smooth. Transfer the mixture to a serving dish, cover, and chill for several hours.

3. Serve with French bread or whole grain crackers.

1 cup dried brown lentils, sorted

2 cups water

¾ cup chopped onion

1 cup chopped fresh mushrooms

1 teaspoon beef or vegetable bouillon granules

¾ teaspoon dried thyme

¼ teaspoon ground allspice

⅛ teaspoon ground black pepper

NUTRITIONAL FACTS (PER TABLESPOON)

Calories: 23	Fat: 0.1 g	Protein: 1.8 g
Cholesterol: 0 mg	Fiber: 0.8 g	Sodium: 33 mg

How to Turn a Cocktail Party Into Dinner

If the host of your next party has not yet switched to a low-fat lifestyle, you will probably be faced with a tempting table of high-fat hors d'oeuvres. Heavy hors d'oeuvres can and should be considered dinner for anyone who's watching his or her waistline. Even then, these appetizing tidbits must be selected properly in order to provide a balanced meal that doesn't quickly outstrip a reasonable allotment of calories and fat. Here are some guidelines:

☐ Begin with an "entrée"----some high-protein appetizers such as cheese cubes or steamed shrimp. Eat in moderation. There's more to come!

☐ A well-balanced meal must include some vegetables, so move on to the vegetable tray for your next course. Try to use a minimal amount of dip, and add some whole grain crackers if available.

☐ Fruit adds refreshing balance to a meal, and has almost no fat, so have a serving or two of melon, pineapple, berries, or other fresh fruits.

☐ For your beverage, pour yourself a glass of club soda or spring water, or choose a diet soft drink. Alcohol is almost as high in calories as those pigs'n'blankets that you love so much!

☐ For dessert, serve yourself a moderate portion of something decadent that you really want. Then enjoy it!

So the next time you're invited to a party, don't despair. You don't have to blow your fat budget in order to enjoy yourself. Just pretend that you've been invited out to dinner, and serve yourself a meal that's high on satisfaction and low on guilt.

Part Two

Traditional Holiday Meals

Whenever we think of Thanksgiving, Christmas, Hanukkah, Easter, and other traditional holidays, a flood of images comes to mind. Beautifully decorated fir trees, the flickering candles of a menorah, rainbow-colored eggs----these symbols are all inextricably linked with the holidays that brighten each calendar year. In fact, Christmas probably wouldn't seem like Christmas without an ornamented tree and gaily wrapped gifts. Just as strong as these images are those of the special foods that are traditionally served for each holiday. Thanksgiving turkey and stuffing, for instance, is a must for most of us. Thanksgiving just wouldn't be the same without it.

Yet, when we make the switch to a more healthful diet, we face a dilemma. How can we enjoy lavish meals of holiday favorites, and still prepare low-fat high-nutrient dishes? Part Two answers this question with inventive menus that combine "defatted" traditional dishes with exciting new fare for festive meals that are sure to delight family and friends.

The holiday season begins with a sumptuous Thanksgiving feast. Roast turkey, of course, takes center stage, accompanied by Foolproof Fat-Free Gravy and any one of four savory stuffings. To round out the meal, choose from among two refreshing cranberry sauces, as well as a bevy of vegetable side dishes and salads, including such favorites as Pineapple-Sweet Potato Casserole and Easy Mashed Potatoes. What's for dessert? Offer guests a choice of two classic Thanksgiving treats. Cool and creamy Baked Pumpkin Custard and hot and bubbly Cranapple Crisp are both delicious and made with absolutely no added fat.

Christmas brings a complete holiday menus. Tired of turkey? This meal pairs pork tenderloins with pineapple stuffing for an outrageously luscious main dish. Surrounding the pork roasts are Parmesan Scalloped Potatoes, Glazed Snow Peas and Carrots, and Cran-Raspberry Ring. Creamy Cherry Cheesecake makes a colorful climax to a festive meal.

Hanukkah poses a special challenge to the fat-free cook. Usually, the Festival of Lights is celebrated with dishes cooked in oil to remind us of the holy oil that burned so long. How can we prepare these time-honored dishes *without* the oil and without sacrificing taste? These menus meet the challenge with both traditional holiday treats and new dishes, all defatted and all delicious.

Our Hanukkah feast begins with Ruby Borscht, a rosy soup garnished with nonfat sour cream and a sprinkling of dill. Following the soup is Roast Turkey Breast With Sourdough Stuffing and Savory Gravy, accompanied by Green Beans and Mushrooms, Sunshine Carrot Salad, and Cranberry Pear Conserve and traditional Potato Latkes. Dessert brings fat-free Festive Noodle Pudding, a creamy confection that may be served hot or cold.

As winter turns to spring, celebrate Passover with meals that marry traditional Passover foods with healthful fat-free ingredients. The Seder menu begins with a Passover must----matzo ball soup. The broth is enriched with sweet potatoes for a golden color and a delightfully different flavor. Braised Beef With Carrots and Prunes, a hearty dish made low-fat by replacing the usual brisket with beef round; Asparagus Vinaigrette; Scalloped Tomato Matzo; and warm Apple Matzo Kugel complete the feast.

Our Easter menu celebrate spring with selections of fresh and flavorful dishes. Creamy Cucumber Dip served with raw vegetables and whole grain crackers makes a light and flavorful beginning. Then comes a marinated tenderloin of pork, fragrant with herbs and spices. Accompanying the entrée are creamy Corn Pudding, Company Carrot-Raisin Salad, and spring-fresh Steamed Asparagus. And the crowning touch to this elegant meal? Chocolate Raspberry Torte, a dessert so rich and extravagant, no one will believe it's fat free!

As you browse through the following menus and recipes to plan your next special-occasion get-together, don't hesitate to mix and match dishes from different menus. Feel free to make the switch! That is why we have presented so many options----so that you can create meals that will best suit your family's tastes and your own style of entertaining. And don't forget that more holiday and party recipes can be found in Parts One, Three, and Four.

So gather family and friends, and get ready to start some new traditions. Holidays are sure to be even more enjoyable when the dishes you serve are not only festive and enticing, but also satisfying, wholesome, and full of the nutrients that insure good health the whole year round.

Surviving the Holiday Season

November and December are difficult months for those of us who are watching our weight. 'Tis the season for family feasts, office parties, and open houses. For two months, we are faced with every culinary temptation imaginable. In fact, it is not unusual for people to gain ten or even twenty pounds between the start of the football season and January 2.

Fortunately, the situation is far from hopeless. It is possible to enjoy all the festivities----including the special foods that help make the season so enjoyable----and still stay within the boundaries of a reasonable diet. So take heart, and use the following strategies to help maintain some semblance of sanity during the festive season.

☐ *Plan ahead.* If you know that you will be going to a party, work it into your daily meal plan. Save one-third to one-fourth of that day's calorie allotment for a cocktail party, and one-third to one-half of your allotment for a dinner party. Avoid going out for dinner after a cocktail party, as you will almost certainly overshoot your food limit for the day. Heavy hors d'oeuvres should be considered dinner. (To learn about turning a cocktail party into dinner, see the inset on page 30.)

☐ *Don't starve yourself.* Going to a party feeling ravenous will most likely cause you to overeat. Don't starve yourself all day in anticipation of the goodies ahead. Instead, eat a light breakfast and lunch, and save some calories for the evening.

☐ *Eat only special foods.* Don't waste fat and calories on ordinary party and snack foods like chips and dips----foods that you can eat any time of the year. Concentrate on foods that are not usually available, and then eat them only in moderation.

☐ *Eat slowly.* By eating slowly, you will feel more satisfied with less food. (After twenty minutes of eating, the body signals a feeling of fullness to the brain.)

☐ *Remember the law of diminishing returns.* The more you eat of something, the less pleasure you receive. For example, that first bite of cheesecake is the best, because the taste is so new. As you continue to eat, the pleasure diminishes. So eat just

a bite or two, and receive 90 percent of the pleasure for only 10 percent of the fat and calories!

☐ *Don't set yourself up for failure.* Make a conscious effort to position yourself away from the hors d'oeuvres. This will prevent you from munching away as you chat with others.

☐ *Beware of the bubbly.* Alcohol contains almost as many calories as fat does. Combine it with creamy or sweet mixers, and you get even more calories. Another problem is that alcohol lowers your inhibitions, possibly making you careless about food choices. What can you do? Sip a wine spritzer, or mix the liquor with water, soda, or a diet beverage. Then alternate alcoholic drinks with glasses of water. Or simply drink club soda or another nonalcoholic beverage instead of the alcohol, and spend more of your calorie budget on delicious holiday foods.

☐ *Enlist the help of others.* No one wants to put on excess pounds during the holidays, so enlist the help of friends, family, and co-workers. You'll then be able to help one another plan more healthful menus and eat within reason.

☐ *Keep things in perspective.* If you lose control at a party or gathering, don't try to make up for it by starving the next day. Instead, get back on track and pick up where you left off. Remember that the most important part of the holidays is time spent with family and friends. Focus on the social aspects, think less about food, and don't punish yourself if you overindulge a little now and then.

Of course, there will be times when you are the host of the party. Make the most of this by serving a selection of healthful fat-free and low-fat foods. In Part One, you'll find dozens of ideas for fat- and calorie-smart appetizers. More healthful holidays recipes can be found throughout Parts Two and Three. Add some trays of fresh fruit and vegetables, as well as plenty of spring water and other low-cal beverages, and you'll set both yourself and your guests up for success instead of failure. Friends and family will appreciate this more than you know.

Thanksgiving

Thanksgiving kicks the holiday season into full swing. For many people, the season brings to mind fond memories of festive feasts----and not-so-fond memories of the resulting extra pounds. Holiday favorites are usually loaded with fat, sugar, and calories. Fortunately, it is possible to reduce the fat and sugar in these foods and still make them every bit as enjoyable as ever. The proof is in the traditional Thanksgiving dinner that follows.

When aiming for fat-free fare, it's hard to go wrong with turkey as a main course. The stuffing and gravy, however, are usually loaded with fat. Here you will find a variety of great-tasting stuffings that are virtually fat-free and full of whole grain goodness. And don't be afraid to pour on Foolproof Fat-Free Gravy!

Accompany the main course with Thanksgiving favorites like Waldorf Salad, Pineapple-Sweet Potato Casserole, Easy Mashed Potatoes, and Broccoli Casserole. Cranberry sauce is a must, and two versions are offered here. Dessert anyone? Try some Baked Pumpkin Custard or Cranapple Crisp. Both contain no added fat and are lower in sugar than traditionally made desserts.

You'll notice that this collection of Thanksgiving dishes is a bit lavish. This is not because we recommend that your Thanksgiving table groan with extra food! Rather, a few extras have been added for variety. Who knows? You may want to prepare a variation of this menu at Christmas time.

Although Thanksgiving dinner is an extravagant meal, the preparations for it need not be overwhelming. Only two dishes must be fully prepared right before serving: the turkey and the mashed potatoes. However, once the turkey is placed in the oven to roast, it will require little of your attention for several hours. And, of course, the mashed potatoes are quite easy to make at the last minute. Or, if you prefer, serve the sweet potato casserole, which can be partially prepared in advance by baking the potatoes the day before. On the day of your dinner, just toss the casserole ingredients together, top with marshmallows, and bake.

If you have chosen a bread-based stuffing, the bread can be cubed and processed into crumbs the day before the dinner, and stored in a plastic bag. Also cut up any vegetables a day in advance, cover, and refrigerate until the next day, to finish the stuffing preparations.

Either of the cranberry sauces can easily be made as much as two days in advance. Cover and chill them, and they'll keep beautifully until serving time.

Cranapple Crisp must, of course, be assembled and baked right before serving time, and then brought to the table hot and bubbly. Either dessert will be a fitting finale to a deliciously traditional feast.

Thanksgiving Dinner

Menu

SERVES 10 TO 12

Roast Turkey (page 72) with Stuffing (page 36)

Foolproof Fat-Free Gravy (page 41)

Waldorf Salad (page 41)

Broccoli Casserole (page 42)

Easy Mashed Potatoes (page 42)
or Pineapple-Sweet Potato Casserole (page 43)

Cranberry Sauce (page 45)

Baked Pumpkin Custard (page 46)
Cranapple Crisp (page 84)

Roast Turkey

Yield: 16 servings

12-pound turkey, fresh or defrosted

½ cup water

½ cup dry sherry

BASTING SAUCE

2 tablespoons dry sherry

1 teaspoon crushed fresh garlic

¼ teaspoon ground black pepper

1 teaspoon poultry seasoning

1½ teaspoons paprika

1 teaspoon brown sugar

NUTRITIONAL FACTS (PER 3-OUNCE SERVING, SKINLESS WHITE MEAT)

Calories: 119	Fiber: 0 g
Chol.: 73 mg	Protein: 26 g
Fat: 1 g	Sodium: 48 mg

NUTRITIONAL FACTS (PER 3-OUNCE SERVING, SKINLESS DARK MEAT)

Calories: 159	Fiber: 0 g
Chol.: 72 mg	Protein: 24 g
Fat: 6 g	Sodium: 67 mg

The method of foil roasting used in this recipe differs from conventional foil-tent roasting in that the bird is totally enclosed in foil for most of the baking time to seal in the moisture. During the last 30 minutes of baking, the foil is removed to allow the skin to brown before serving.

1. Remove the package containing the giblets and neck from the cavities of the turkey. (You may have to release the legs from a band of skin or a wire or plastic lock in order to remove the giblets and neck.) Rinse the turkey, inside and out, and dry it with paper towels. Trim off any excess fat.

2. Transfer the turkey to a rack in a large roasting pan. Return the legs to the wire or plastic lock or band of skin, or loosely tie the legs together with a cord. Fold the wings back and underneath the bird.

3. Pour the water and sherry into the bottom of the roasting pan. Combine the basting sauce ingredients in a small bowl, and brush the sauce over the skin of the bird. Completely enclose the bird in aluminum foil, crimping the foil around the edges of the pan to seal.

4. Bake at 325°F for 3¼ to 4 hours. During the last 30 minutes of cooking, remove the foil and baste with the pan juices.

5. When the turkey is done, a thermometer inserted in the thigh will read 180°F to 185°F, and the drumsticks will move easily in the sockets. Remove the turkey from the oven, and allow it to sit, loosely covered with foil, for 20 minutes before carving.

Savory Stuffings

Nearly every family has its favorite stuffing recipe. The problem is that whether your family's stuffing is savory with sage or sweet with apples and raisins, it's probably also loaded with fat. Fortunately, it is possible to make stuffing that's flavorful and moist while being virtually fat-free. In fact, the following stuffings are so delicious that you may decide to make them part of your daily fare, rather than reserving them for festive occasions.

For safety's sake, it is best to cook the stuffing outside of the bird. Why? Stuffing, improperly handled, is a perfect breeding ground for the harmful bacteria sometimes found in poultry. For this reason, all of the stuffings presented here are baked in casserole dishes. If you choose to bake your stuffing *inside* the bird, omit the broth or Butter Buds liquid used to moisten the stuffing, as the juices from the bird will make the added liquid unnecessary. Always stuff the turkey right before roasting, and be sure to stuff it loosely, leaving a little space at the end for expansion. After spooning in the stuffing, secure the turkey's legs and wings, as explained in the turkey recipe, and cook thoroughly. The internal temperature of the stuffing should reach 165°F. Then remove the stuffing from the bird directly after roasting, and enjoy!

Cranberry-Wild Rice Stuffing

Yield: 12 servings

1. Combine all of the ingredients except for the cranberry sauce in a 2½-quart pot. Bring the mixture to a boil over high heat. Reduce the heat to low, cover, and simmer without stirring for 45 to 50 minutes, or until the liquid has been absorbed. Remove the pot from the heat, and set aside, uncovered, for 5 minutes.

2. Coat a 2-quart casserole dish with nonstick cooking spray. Stir the cranberry sauce into the stuffing mixture, and loosely spoon the stuffing into the dish. Cover the dish with aluminum foil, and bake at 350°F for 30 to 45 minutes, or until heated through. Serve hot.

1 cup uncooked brown rice

½ cup uncooked wild rice

1 medium onion, chopped

1 cup thinly sliced celery (include leaves)

1 bay leaf

1 teaspoon dried rosemary, or 1 tablespoon fresh

3 cups unsalted chicken broth or water

1 teaspoon chicken bouillon granules

¼ teaspoon ground white pepper

1 cup whole berry cranberry sauce

NUTRITIONAL FACTS (PER ½-CUP SERVING)

Calories: 121	Fat: 0.5 g	Protein: 24 g
Cholesterol: 0 mg	Fiber: 2 g	Sodium: 103 mg

Sage and Herb Whole Wheat Stuffing

Yield: 12 servings

12 slices stale whole wheat bread

1 medium onion, finely chopped

1 cup finely chopped celery (include leaves)

1 teaspoon dried sage

¾ teaspoon dried thyme

¾ teaspoon dried marjoram

¼ teaspoon ground black pepper

2 egg whites, lightly beaten (optional)

⅔ cup chicken broth or Butter Buds liquid

1. Take 8 of the 12 slices of bread, and tear them into small pieces. Place the pieces in a food processor or blender, and process into coarse crumbs. Measure the crumbs. There should be 4 cups. (Adjust the amount if necessary.)

2. Take the remaining 4 slices of bread, and cut the bread into ½-inch cubes. Measure the cubes. There should be 4 cups. (Adjust the amount if necessary.)

3. Place the bread crumbs and cubes in a large bowl, and add all of the remaining ingredients except for the chicken broth. Toss to mix well. Slowly add the broth as you continue tossing.

4. Coat a 2-quart casserole dish with nonstick cooking spray. Loosely spoon the stuffing into the dish, and bake uncovered at 325°F for 45 minutes to an hour, or until heated through and lightly browned on top. Serve hot.

NUTRITIONAL FACTS (PER ½-CUP SERVING)

Calories: 92	Fat: 1 g	Protein: 3.7 g
Cholesterol: 0 mg	Fiber: 2.5 g	Sodium: 205 mg

Variations

For a change of pace, add one of the following ingredients to your whole wheat stuffing:

- 1 cup peeled chopped roasted chestnuts
- 1 can (8 ounces) chopped mushrooms, drained, or 1½ cups chopped fresh mushrooms, sautéed in 1 tablespoon of chicken broth

Apple-Raisin Stuffing

Yield: 12 servings

1. Take 6 of the 9 slices of bread, and tear them into small pieces. Place the pieces in a food processor or blender, and process into coarse crumbs. Measure the crumbs. There should be 3 cups. (Adjust the amount if necessary.)

2. Take the remaining 3 slices of bread, and cut them into ½-inch cubes. Measure the cubes. There should be 3 cups. (Adjust the amount if necessary.)

3. Place the bread crumbs and cubes in a large bowl, and add all of the remaining ingredients except for the chicken broth. Toss to mix well. Slowly add the broth as you continue tossing.

4. Coat a 2-quart casserole dish with nonstick cooking spray. Loosely spoon the stuffing into the dish, and bake uncovered at 325°F for 45 minutes to an hour, or until heated through and lightly browned on top. Serve hot.

9 slices stale whole wheat bread

3 large tart apples, peeled and coarsely chopped

¾ cup dark or golden raisins

1 cup finely chopped celery (include leaves)

½ cup finely chopped onion

1 teaspoon poultry seasoning

¼ teaspoon ground white pepper

½ cup chopped walnuts or pecans (optional)

2 egg whites, lightly beaten (optional)

½ cup chicken broth or Butter Buds liquid

NUTRITIONAL FACTS (PER ½-CUP SERVING)

Calories: 119	Fat: 0.7 g	Protein: 3.2 g
Cholesterol: 0 mg	Fiber: 2.9 g	Sodium: 181 mg

Old-Fashioned Cornbread Dressing

Yield: 12 servings

1 cup chopped onion

1 cup thinly sliced celery (include leaves)

1½ teaspoons dried sage

1 teaspoon poultry seasoning

¼ teaspoon ground black pepper

⅔ cup chicken broth or Butter Buds liquid

2 egg whites, lightly beaten (optional)

CORNBREAD

1½ cups whole grain cornmeal

2 teaspoons baking powder

4 egg whites, lightly beaten

1¼ cups nonfat buttermilk

1 teaspoon butter-flavored extract

1. To make the cornbread, combine the cornmeal and baking powder in a large bowl, and stir to mix well. Add the remaining cornbread ingredients, and stir to mix well.

2. Coat a 9-inch square pan with nonstick cooking spray. Spread the batter evenly in the pan, and bake at 400°F for 20 to 25 minutes, or until a wooden toothpick inserted in the center of the bread comes out clean and the bread begins to pull slightly from the sides of the pan. Cool completely.

3. Remove the cornbread from the pan, and crumble into a large bowl. Add the remaining ingredients, and toss to mix well.

4. Coat a 2-quart casserole dish with nonstick cooking spray. Loosely spoon the stuffing into the dish, and bake uncovered at 325°F for 45 minutes to an hour, or until heated through and lightly browned on top. Serve hot.

NUTRITIONAL FACTS (PER ½-CUP SERVING)

Calories: 77	Fat: 0.8 g	Protein: 3.5 g
Cholesterol: 0 mg	Fiber: 2 g	Sodium: 107 mg

Time-Saving Tip

To make Thanksgiving Day a little less hectic, bake the cornbread 1 to 3 days in advance. Then complete the stuffing preparations the day before or the morning of the dinner, and pop the casserole into the oven 1 hour before serving time.

Variation

To make Country Sausage Stuffing, cook 8 ounces of ground turkey breakfast sausage in a nonstick skillet, stirring constantly to crumble. Drain the sausage, and add it to the stuffing mixture.

Foolproof Fat-Free Gravy

1. Defat the pan drippings by placing them in a fat separator cup. (If you don't have a separator cup, pour the drippings into a bowl, add a few ice cubes, and skim off the fat once it rises and hardens.) Combine the fat-free drippings, pepper, poultry seasoning, and bouillon granules in a 1-quart saucepan, and simmer over low heat for 5 minutes.

2. While the gravy is heating, combine the flour and milk in a jar with a tight-fitting lid, and shake until smooth. Slowly add the milk mixture to the simmering broth, stirring constantly with a wire whisk. Continue to cook and stir until the gravy is thick and bubbly.

3. Transfer the gravy to a warmed gravy boat or pitcher, and serve hot with the turkey.

Yield: 2½ cups

2 cups turkey drippings

⅛ teaspoon ground white pepper

¼ teaspoon poultry seasoning

1 teaspoon chicken bouillon granules

¼ cup plus 1 tablespoon unbleached flour

½ cup skim milk

NUTRITIONAL FACTS (PER TABLESPOON)

Calories: 7	Fat: 0 g	Protein: 0.4 g
Cholesterol: 0 mg	Fiber: 0 g	Sodium: 25 mg

Waldorf Salad

1. In a large bowl, combine the apples, celery, raisins, and walnuts, and stir to mix well.

2. In a small bowl, combine the mayonnaise with the sour cream, and stir to mix well. Add the mayonnaise mixture to the apple mixture, and toss to mix.

3. Cover the salad and chill for 1 to 3 hours before serving.

Yield: 12 servings

6 cups diced apples

2½ cups thinly sliced celery

¼ cup plus 2 tablespoons dark raisins

⅓ cup chopped walnuts (optional)

DRESSING

¼ cup plus 2 tablespoons nonfat or reduced-fat mayonnaise

¼ cup plus 2 tablespoons nonfat sour cream

NUTRITIONAL FACTS (PER ⅔-CUP SERVING)

Calories: 63	Fat: 0.2 g	Protein: 1 g
Cholesterol: 0 mg	Fiber: 2 g	Sodium: 94 mg

Broccoli Casserole

Yield: 12 servings

1½ cups shredded nonfat or reduced-fat sharp Cheddar cheese

2 packages (10 ounces each) frozen chopped broccoli, thawed and drained

⅓ cup finely chopped onion

⅓ cup fat-free egg substitute

1¾ cups dry curd or nonfat cottage cheese

2 tablespoons unbleached flour

¼ teaspoon ground white pepper

3 tablespoons finely ground fat-free cracker crumbs

1. Set aside ½ cup of the grated Cheddar cheese. Combine the rest of the cheese and all of the remaining ingredients except for the cracker crumbs in a large bowl, and stir to mix well.

2. Coat a 2½-quart casserole dish with nonstick cooking spray. Place the broccoli mixture in the dish, sprinkle with the cracker crumbs, and spread the reserved cheese over the top.

3. Bake at 350°F for 50 minutes, or until the top is golden brown. Let sit for 5 minutes before serving.

NUTRITIONAL FACTS (PER ⅔-CUP SERVING)

Calories: 68   Fat: 0.2 g   Protein: 10 g
Cholesterol: 3 mg   Fiber: 1.8 g   Sodium: 147 mg

Easy Mashed Potatoes

Yield: 12 servings

8 medium potatoes

½ cup nonfat dry milk powder

3 tablespoons butter-flavored sprinkles

¼ teaspoon ground white pepper

1. Peel the potatoes, and cut them into chunks. Place the potatoes in a 4-quart pot, and add water just to cover. Bring the potatoes to a boil over high heat. Reduce the heat to medium, cover, and cook for 10 minutes, or until the potatoes are soft.

2. Drain all but about ⅔ cup of water from the pot, reserving the drained water. Add the dry milk powder, butter-flavored sprinkles, and pepper to the potatoes, and mash them with a potato masher until smooth. If the potatoes are too stiff, add a little of the reserved cooking liquid. Serve immediately.

NUTRITIONAL FACTS (PER 1/2-CUP SERVING)

Calories: 96   Fat: 0.1 g   Protein: 2.8 g
Cholesterol: 0 mg   Fiber: 1.5 g   Sodium: 86 mg

A Tempting Selection of Hot Hors D'Oeuvres
Top: Spicy Barbecue Meatballs (page 18)
Center Left: Flaky Spinach Pies (page 23)
Center Right: Florentine Stuffed Mushrooms (page 19)
Bottom: Bacon Wrapped Shrimp (page 19)

A Variety of Festive Cold Hors D'Oeuvres
Top: Salmon Mousse (page 26)
Bottom Left: High Rollers (page 25)
Bottom Right: Creamy Cucumber Dip (page 26)

Thanksgiving Turkey and Fixings
Top: Roast Turkey (page 36)
Center Left: Broccoli Casserole (page 42)
Center Right: Old-Fashioned Cornbread Dressing (page 40)
Bottom: Waldorf Salad (page 41)

Thanksgiving Side Dishes
Top Left: Pineapple-Sweet Potato Casserole (page 43)
Top Right: Cranberry-Wild Rice Stuffing (page 37)
Bottom: Molded Cranberry-Apple Relish (page 45)

A Merry Christmas Dinner
Top Left: Parmesan Scalloped Potatoes (page 50)
Top Right: Glazed Snow Peas and Carrots (page 50)
Bottom: Pork Tenderloins With Pineapple Stuffing (page 49)

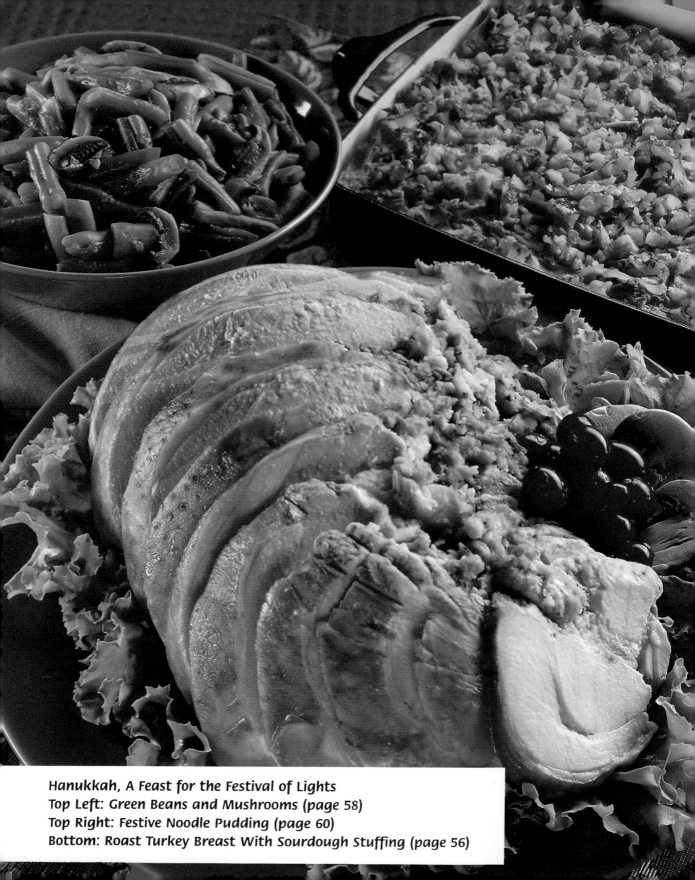

Hanukkah, A Feast for the Festival of Lights
Top Left: Green Beans and Mushrooms (page 58)
Top Right: Festive Noodle Pudding (page 60)
Bottom: Roast Turkey Breast With Sourdough Stuffing (page 56)

Variation

For a different taste, make Easy Mashed Potatoes with nonfat sour cream or plain nonfat yogurt instead of nonfat dry milk. Just omit the dry milk, and drain all of the liquid from the potatoes. Add ¾ cup of nonfat sour cream or yogurt, and mash as directed. If the potatoes seem too stiff, return a little of the reserved cooking liquid to the pot.

Pineapple-Sweet Potato Casserole

Yield: 12 servings

3 pounds sweet potatoes (about 6 medium-large)

2 cans (8 ounces each) crushed pineapple in juice, undrained

¼ teaspoon ground cinnamon

4 teaspoons butter-flavored sprinkles

⅓ cup chopped pecans or golden raisins (optional)

1¾ cups miniature marshmallows

1. To cook the sweet potatoes in a conventional oven, bake them at 400°F for about 45 minutes, or until tender. To cook in a microwave oven, prick each potato in several places with a fork, and microwave at high power for about 15 minutes, or until tender. Set aside to cool; then peel and cut into bite-sized pieces.

2. Place the potato pieces in a large bowl and toss with all of the remaining ingredients except the marshmallows. Coat a 2½-quart casserole dish with nonstick cooking spray, and place the sweet potato mixture in the dish. Top with the marshmallows.

3. Bake at 350°F for 35 to 40 minutes, or until the sweet potato mixture is bubbly and the top is lightly browned. If the top starts to brown too quickly, loosely cover the dish with aluminum foil during the last 10 minutes of baking. Serve hot.

NUTRITIONAL FACTS (PER ½-CUP SERVING)

Calories: 143	Fat: 0.2 g	Protein: 2 g
Cholesterol: 0 mg	Fiber: 2.5 g	Sodium: 65 mg

Time-Saving Tip

Instead of using fresh potatoes, use 3 pounds of canned sweet potatoes. Just drain and slice the potatoes, and use them as you would the cut-up baked potatoes.

Trimming the Fat
From Your Thanksgiving Feast

If you look back at holiday dinners past, it's easy to see why we all gain weight during this festive time of year. At Thanksgiving alone, the parade of tempting dishes often begins even before dinner with several appetizers, perhaps accompanied by wine. Then comes the turkey and possibly a ham. With the turkey is served three or four different starches----stuffing, mashed potatoes, sweet potatoes, and rolls, for instance----as well as two or more vegetables and, of course, cranberry sauce. Naturally, the turkey, stuffing, and potatoes are topped with fat-laden gravy. And the whole meal is topped with a selection of rich desserts. Even if you insist on fairly small portions, you're likely to use up an entire day's calorie allotment on a dinner like this. You're also likely to feel uncomfortably full at meal's end.

However, it really is possible to enjoy Thanksgiving and other holidays and still eat healthfully. Realize that holiday meals can be a lot simpler than they usually are, but every bit as enjoyable and well-balanced. For instance, roast turkey with stuffing and gravy, along with one other starch----either sweet potatoes or mashed potatoes, for instance----a salad, a vegetable, and dessert make a well-balanced and satisfying meal.

What can you do about all those fat-laden holiday recipes? Keep them, but give them slimming makeovers. Here are some ideas for trimming the fat from your Thanksgiving feast:

☐ Turkey is an ideal low-fat main course. To help keep it this way, buy a fresh unbasted turkey instead of the pre-basted kind, which has been injected with a mixture of oil and salty broth. (Read the label to see if it's been pre-basted.) Then examine the turkey for extra fat, and trim it away.

☐ Baste your turkey with broth, sherry, or white wine instead of fat. During cooking, cover the turkey with foil to retain moistness. Then uncover the bird during the last 30 minutes so that it turns a beautiful brown.

☐ When making your gravy, pour the pan juices into a fat separator cup. This specially designed device has a spout that goes to the bottom of the cup, allowing you to pour off just the broth while the fat, which has risen to the top, stays in the cup. If you don't have a separator cup, pour the juices into a bowl, and add a few ice cubes. The fat will then rise to the top and harden, where it can be easily skimmed off.

☐ Moisten your dressing with broth instead of fat. For added nutrition, try using whole wheat bread instead of white. Then, instead of using salt for flavor, add lots of celery, onion, and other vegetables, as well as herbs and spices.

☐ Get the fat out of side dishes and casseroles. For example, make your mashed potatoes with butter-flavored sprinkles and skim milk, nonfat yogurt, or nonfat sour cream. When making casseroles, use nonfat cheeses, nonfat sour cream, and low-fat cream soups. Lighten your salads with nonfat mayonnaise, nonfat sour cream, and fat-free salad dressings.

☐ Modify your holiday dessert recipes. For instance, use evaporated skim milk in pumpkin pies; substitute egg whites for whole eggs; and reduce the sugar by 25 percent. Choose fruit-based desserts like cobblers and fruit crisps over gooey cakes and pastries.

As you can see, it's not difficult to make a Thanksgiving dinner that is both satisfying and healthful. By trimming the fat from your favorite holiday dishes----and by trimming away any extra dishes, as well----you will surpise both yourself and your family with a memorable feast that is also low in fat and high in nutrition.

Molded Cranberry-Apple Relish

1. Combine the gelatin mix and brown sugar in a large heat-proof bowl. Add the boiling water, and stir until the mix is dissolved. Cover and chill for about 45 minutes, or until the mixture has thickened to the consistency of raw egg whites.

2. Stir the remaining ingredients into the gelatin mixture. Pour the mixture into an ungreased 6-cup mold, cover, and chill for 6 to 8 hours, or until very firm.

3. To unmold the relish, dip the mold in warm----but not hot----water for 5 to 10 seconds. Beware: If the water is too hot or the mold remains in the water too long, the gelatin will start to melt. Remove the mold from the water and loosen the edges of the mixture with a knife. Place a serving platter upside down over the mold, and invert the mold onto the platter. Slice and serve chilled.

Yield: 12 servings

1 package (4-serving size) sugar-free black raspberry gelatin mix

¼ cup light brown sugar

1½ cups boiling water

1½ cups fresh or frozen cranberries, stemmed and coarsely chopped

1 medium apple, peeled and finely chopped

½ cup finely chopped celery

⅓ cup chopped pecans (optional)

NUTRITIONAL FACTS (PER ⅓-CUP SERVING)

Calories: 30   Fat: 0.1 g
Cholesterol: 0 mg Protein:0.5g
Fiber: 0.9g   Sodium: 23 mg

Orange-Cranberry Sauce

1. Combine the orange juice, orange rind, and brown sugar in a 2-quart pot, and stir to mix well. Place over medium heat, and bring to a boil, stirring constantly. Stop stirring, and allow the mixture to boil for 5 minutes with the pot uncovered.

2. Add the cranberries to the pot, and stir to mix. Simmer the mixture over medium heat, with the cover of the pot on but ajar, for 7 to 10 minutes, or until the cranberry skins pop open. Stir occasionally.

3. Allow the mixture to cool to room temperature. Transfer to a serving bowl, cover, and chill for at least 4 hours before serving.

Yeild: 12 Servings

1 cup orange juice
1/2 tablespoon freshly grated orange rind, or 1/2 teaspoon dried

1/2 cup brown sugar

12 ounces (3 cups) fresh or frozen cranberries, stemmed

NUTRITIONAL FACTS (PER ⅓-CUP SERVING)

Calories: 30   Fat: 0.1 g
Cholesterol: 0 mg Protein:0.5g
Fiber: 0.9g   Sodium: 23 mg

Baked Pumpkin Custard

Yield: 8 servings

1½ cups canned or mashed
   cooked pumpkin

1 can (12 ounces) evaporated
   skim milk

1¾ cups fat-free egg substitute

⅓ cup orange juice

1½ teaspoons vanilla extract

½ cup light brown sugar

1½ teaspoons pumpkin pie spice

1. Place all of the ingredients in a blender or food processor, and process until smooth.

2. Coat a 2-quart soufflé dish with nonstick cooking spray. Pour the mixture into the dish, and place the dish in a pan filled with 1 inch of hot water.

3. Bake at 350°F for about 1 hour and 15 minutes, or until a sharp knife inserted in the center of the custard comes out clean. Chill for at least 8 hours or overnight and serve.

NUTRITIONAL FACTS (PER ⅔-CUP SERVING)

Calories: 131	Fat: 0.2 g	Protein: 8.6 g
Cholesterol: 0 mg	Fiber: 0.9 g	Sodium: 131 mg

Cranapple Crisp

Yield: 8 servings

FRUIT FILLING

8 cups thinly sliced peeled apples

½ cup fresh or frozen cranberries,
   coarsely chopped

⅓ cup light brown sugar

¼ cup golden raisins

1 tablespoon cornstarch

1 tablespoon apple juice
   concentrate, thawed

TOPPING

⅔ cup quick-cooking oats

3 tablespoons whole wheat flour

¼ cup light brown sugar

¼ teaspoon ground cinnamon

2 tablespoons frozen apple juice
   concentrate, thawed

1. To make the topping, in a small bowl, combine the oats, flour, sugar, and cinnamon, and stir to mix well. Add the juice concentrate, and stir until moist and crumbly. Set aside.

2. In a large bowl, combine the filling ingredients, and toss to mix well. Coat a 2½-quart casserole dish with nonstick cooking spray. Place the filling mixture in the dish, and sprinkle with the topping.

3. Bake at 375°F for 30 minutes. Cover the dish loosely with foil, and bake for an additional 15 minutes, or until the filling is bubbly and the topping is golden brown. Serve warm.

NUTRITIONAL FACTS (PER ¾-CUP SERVING)

Calories: 178	Fat: 0.7 g	Protein: 1.7 g
Cholesterol: 0 mg	Fiber: 4 g	Sodium: 7 mg

Christmas

As visions of sugarplums dance in our heads, so perhaps do less-pleasant visions of heavy, diet-busting holiday roasts, side dishes, and desserts. Ready for a change of pace? Then delight guests with our light and delicious Christmas Dinner.

Perhaps you're all turkeyed out after Thanksgiving. In that case, our Christmas menu may be just what you're looking for.

Begin the festivities with an elegant appetizer of warm artichoke hearts marinated in a tangy mustard sauce and wrapped in ultra-lean ham. Then serve your main dish, which pairs the leanest and most tender cut of pork available with a pineapple-bread stuffing to create an entrée that is as attractive as it is delicious. Accompanying the pork and stuffing is a creamy yet fat-free version of Scalloped Potatoes, festive Glazed Snow Peas and Carrots, and colorful molded Cran-Raspberry Ring. For dessert, indulge in guilt-free Creamy Cherry Cheesecake. Made with nonfat cheeses, this deceptively rich confection has the smoothness of traditional cheesecake with none of the traditional fat.

This menu, will enable you to get a head start on meal preparations. The day before your dinner, begin making your appetizer by placing the artichokes in the marinade. On the morning of your party, assemble the dish to the point of

baking. Then pop these savory morsels into the oven just as guests arrive.

Also prepare the bread crumbs and cubes for your stuffing the day before your dinner, and store them in plastic bags until needed. At the same time, chop the vegetables for the stuffing, and store them in the refrigerator. Then, on the evening before or the morning of the party, prepare the tenderloins to the point of baking, cover, and chill. Remove your entrée from the refrigerator about thirty minutes before baking, and place it in the oven until done.

Parmesan Scalloped Potatoes must be assembled just before baking. However, this simple recipe is a snap to put together, and requires little attention once in the oven. You can, of course, cut up the vegetables for the Glazed Snow Peas and Carrots the day before your dinner. Just cover the peas and carrots and store them in the refrigerator until you're ready to complete the dish.

Both the Cran-Raspberry Ring and the Creamy Cherry Cheescake are boons to the make-ahead cook. In fact, both *must* be made the day before your party. Unmold the Cran-Raspberry Ring onto a platter directly before serving, and arrange the grapes around the ring. When it's time to serve the cheesecake, just release the sides from the springform pan. Serving a crowd-pleasing dessert was never simpler!

Christmas Dinner

Menu

SERVES 8 TO 10

Hot Artichoke Appetizers (page 21)

Pork Tenderloins
With Pineapple Stuffing (page 49)

Glazed Snow Peas and Carrots (page 50)

Parmesan Scalloped Potatoes (page 50)

Cran-Raspberry Ring (page 51)

Creamy Cherry Cheesecake (page 52)

Pork Tenderloins With Pineapple Stuffing

Yield: 12 servings

3 pork tenderloins, 1 pound each

PINEAPPLE STUFFING

6 slices cracked wheat or multigrain bread

½ cup crushed pineapple in juice, drained

½ cup chopped water chestnuts

½ cup finely chopped onion

½ cup finely chopped celery

¾ teaspoon dried sage

½ teaspoon poultry seasoning

2 egg whites, lightly beaten

BASTING SAUCE

3 tablespoons unsweetened pineapple juice

3 tablespoons brown sugar

1 tablespoon spicy mustard

1. To make the stuffing, tear 4 of the 6 slices of bread into pieces. Place the pieces in a food processor or blender, and process into coarse crumbs. Measure the crumbs. There should be 2 cups. (Adjust the amount if necessary.) Cut the remaining bread into ½-inch cubes, and measure the cubes. There should be 2 cups. (Adjust the amount if necessary.)

2. Place the bread crumbs and cubes in a medium-sized bowl, and add the crushed pineapple, water chestnuts, onion, celery, and seasonings. Toss to mix well. Add the egg whites, and toss to mix well. Set aside.

3. Combine all of the basting sauce ingredients in a small bowl, and stir to mix well. Set aside.

4. Trim the tenderloins of any visible fat and membranes. Rinse with cool water, and pat dry with paper towels. Split each of the tenderloins lengthwise, cutting not quite all the way through, so that each tenderloin can be spread open like a book. Spread ⅓ of the stuffing mixture over half of each tenderloin, extending the stuffing all the way to the outer edges of the meat. Fold the facing half of each tenderloin over the stuffing-spread half, and use a heavy string to tie the meat together at 2½-inch intervals.

5. Coat a 13-x-16-inch roasting pan with nonstick cooking spray, and lay the tenderloins in the pan, spacing them about 2 inches apart. Bake at 350°F for about 50 minutes, or until the meat is no longer pink inside, occasionally basting with the prepared sauce.

6. Remove the pan from the oven, cover loosely with aluminum foil, and let sit for 5 to 10 minutes before slicing ½ inch thick. Serve immediately.

NUTRITIONAL FACTS (PER 4-OUNCE SERVING)

Calories: 196	Fat: 4.7 g	Protein: 26 g
Cholesterol: 67 mg	Fiber: 1.2 g	Sodium: 147 mg

Glazed Snow Peas and Carrots

Yield: 10 servings

1 teaspoon crushed fresh garlic

1½ teaspoons freshly grated ginger root, or ½ teaspoon ground ginger

4 cups (about 1 pound) snow peas or sugar snap peas

4 cups (about 4 large) diagonally sliced carrots

¼ cup dry sherry or chicken broth

GLAZE

¼ cup chicken broth

2 tablespoons lemon juice

1 tablespoon reduced-sodium soy sauce

2 teaspoons sugar

2 teaspoons cornstarch

1. Combine the glaze ingredients in a small bowl, and stir to mix well. Set aside.

2. Coat a large skillet with nonstick cooking spray, and preheat over medium heat. Place the garlic and ginger in the skillet, and stir-fry for 30 seconds. Add the peas and carrots to the skillet, and pour the sherry or chicken broth over the top. Reduce the heat to medium-low, cover, and cook for 8 to 10 minutes, or until the vegetables are crisp-tender. Stir occasionally.

3. Reduce the heat under the skillet to low. Stir the glaze mixture, and pour over the vegetables. Stirring constantly, cook the vegetable mixture for a minute or 2, until the glaze has thickened. Serve immediately.

NUTRITIONAL FACTS (PER ⅔-CUP SERVING)

Calories: 46	Fat: 0.2 g	Protein: 1.9 g
Cholesterol: 0 mg	Fiber: 2.4 g	Sodium: 89 mg

Parmesan Scalloped Potatoes

Yield: 10 servings

¼ cup unbleached flour

2 tablespoons finely chopped fresh parsley, or 2 teaspoons dried

⅛ teaspoon ground white pepper

2 pounds baking potatoes (about 6 medium)

2 small yellow onions, thinly sliced and separated into rings

½ cup grated nonfat or reduced-fat Parmesan cheese

2 cups evaporated skim milk

1. Combine the flour, parsley, and pepper in a small bowl, and set aside.

2. Scrub the potatoes, and slice them thinly (slightly less than ¼ inch). Measure the potatoes. There should be 6 cups. (Adjust the amount if necessary.)

3. Coat an 8-x-12-inch baking dish with nonstick cooking spray. Arrange 2 cups of the potatoes in a single layer over the bottom of the dish, slightly overlapping the slices. Lay half of the onion rings over the potatoes, and sprinkle the onions with half of the flour mixture and 2 tablespoons of the Parmesan. Repeat these layers, and top with the remaining 2 cups of potatoes. Pour the milk over the potatoes, and sprinkle with the remaining ¼ cup of Parmesan.

4. Cover the dish with aluminum foil, and bake at 350°F for 45 minutes. Remove the foil, and bake for 30 additional minutes, or until the potatoes are tender and the top is golden brown. Remove the dish from the oven, and let sit for 5 minutes before serving.

NUTRITIONAL FACTS (PER ¾-CUP SERVING)

Calories: 168   Fiber: 2.6 g
Cholesterol: 5 mg Protein: 8.1 g
Fat: 0.3 g   Sodium: 103 mg

Cran-Raspberry Ring

1. To make the first layer, combine the sugar and gelatin in a medium-sized heat-proof bowl, and stir to mix well. Place the juice in a small pot, and heat to boiling. Pour the hot juice over the gelatin mixture, and stir until dissolved. Cool to room temperature, and stir in the fruits. Pour the mixture into a 6-cup ring mold, and chill for several hours, or until firm.

2. To make the second layer, place the gelatin in a medium-sized heat-proof bowl. Place the juice in a small pot, and heat to boiling. Pour the hot juice over the gelatin, and stir until dissolved. Cool to room temperature, and stir in the sour cream. Pour the mixture over the first layer in the mold, and chill for several hours, or until firm.

3. To unmold the ring, dip the mold in warm----but not hot----water for 5 to 10 seconds. Beware: If the water is too hot or the mold remains in the water too long, the gelatin will start to melt. Remove the mold from the water and loosen the edges of the mixture with a knife. Place a serving platter upside down over the mold, and invert the mold onto the platter. Arrange some of the grapes in the center of the ring, and the rest around the outer edges of the ring. Slice and serve chilled.

Variation

For a change of pace, substitute strawberry or cherry gelatin for the raspberry gelatin, and strawberries or pitted sweet cherries for the raspberries.

Yield: 10 servings

FIRST LAYER

¼ cup sugar

1 package (4-serving size) sugar-free raspberry gelatin mix

1¼ cups cranberry juice cocktail

1 cup finely chopped fresh or frozen cranberries, stemmed

1 cup finely chopped fresh or frozen raspberries

SECOND LAYER

1 package (4-serving size) sugar-free raspberry gelatin mix

1 cup cranberry juice cocktail

1 cup nonfat sour cream

1¼ pounds seedless green grapes

NUTRITIONAL FACTS (PER ½ CUP GELATIN PLUS ⅓ CUP GRAPES)

Calories: 123   Fiber: 1.2 g
Cholesterol: 0 mg Protein: 3 g
Fat: 0.4 g   Sodium: 62 mg

Creamy Cherry Cheesecake

Yield: 12 servings

CRUST

8 large (2½-x-5-inch) fat-free graham crackers

2 tablespoons sugar

2 tablespoons fat-free egg substitute

FILLING

15 ounces nonfat ricotta cheese

12 ounces nonfat or reduced-fat cream cheese

½ cup fat-free egg substitute

⅓ cup unbleached flour

¾ cup sugar

2 teaspoons vanilla extract

1 tablespoon lemon juice

TOPPING

1½ cups canned light (low-sugar) cherry pie filling

If you are unable to find fat-free graham crackers, feel free to substitute regular graham crackers. All are relatively low in fat.

1. To make the crust, break the crackers into pieces. Place the broken crackers in the bowl of a food processor or in a blender, and process into fine crumbs. Measure the crumbs. There should be 1¼ cups. (Adjust the amount if necessary.)

2. Return the crumbs to the food processor, and add the sugar and the egg substitute. Process until the mixture is moist and crumbly.

3. Coat a 9-inch springform pan with nonstick cooking spray. Use the back of a spoon to press the crumbs over the bottom of the pan and ½ inch up the sides. Periodically dip the spoon in sugar to prevent sticking.

4. Bake the crust at 350°F for 8 minutes, or until the edges feel firm and dry. Cool the crust to room temperature.

5. Place all of the filling ingredients in a food processor, and process until smooth. Pour the filling into the crust, and bake at 325°F for about 55 minutes, or until the center feels firm when lightly touched. Turn the oven off, and let the cake cool in the oven with the door ajar for 1 hour. (The top will crack slightly during cooling.)

6. Spread the cherry filling over the top of the cooled cake to within ¾ inch of the edges. Refrigerate overnight, cut into wedges, and serve.

NUTRITIONAL FACTS (PER SERVING)

Calories: 205	Fat: 0.4 g	Protein: 12.6 g
Cholesterol: 10 mg	Fiber: 0.7 g	Sodium: 299 mg

Hanukkah

Eight days of Hanukkah means lots of friends, family, and good food. The Hanukkah menu presented here provide something for everyone with both traditional holiday treats and some new dishes, all made *without* the traditional fat.

.Our Hanukkah menu is a delight to the eye as well as the taste buds. The celebration begins with a lovely Ruby Borscht, topped with nonfat sour cream and a sprinkling of fresh dill. Serve a crusty loaf of warm sourdough bread alongside, if desired. The main course, Roast Turkey Breast With Sourdough Stuffing and Savory Gravy, also makes a striking appearance, as do the accompanying dishes of Green Beans and Mushrooms, Sunshine Carrot Salad, and Cranberry-Pear Conserve. Accompanying the entrée are Potato Latkes, which are cooked with nonstick cooking spray rather than oil, butter, or chicken fat, and topped with Chunky Applesauce For dessert, bring out Festive Noodle Pudding. Loaded with apples, cranberries, and raisins, and crowned with nuts, this creamy pudding is sure to become a family tradition.

Get an early start on this meal by making the Ruby Borscht the day before the holiday. Refrigerate it until it's time to reheat it on the stove. This rosy soup is even better the next day.

The turkey for this menu's spectacular entrée can be deboned the day before. Also prepare the bread crumbs and cubes and the vegetables for the stuffing in advance, and store them until the day of the dinner, when you will complete the roast preparations.

Rinse and cut the green beans for Green Beans and Mushrooms a day ahead of time. If you purchase mushrooms that are already sliced, this dish can be put together in no time at all.

Both Sunshine Carrot Salad and Cranberry-Pear Conserve should be made in advance to allow the flavors to mingle. Prepare these dishes at least several hours before your dinner, or as early as the previous day.

Finally, fully prepare Festive Noodle Pudding a day in advance, cover the baking dish with aluminum foil, and chill until the afternoon of your dinner. Then bring the pudding to room temperature, or warm it in a 350°F oven for 20 minutes, and serve.

Hanukkah Dinner

Menu

SERVES 10 TO 12

Ruby Borscht (page 55)

*Roast Turkey Breast
With Sourdough Stuffing* (page 56)

Savory Gravy (page 57)

Potato Latkes (page 59)

Green Beans and Mushrooms (page 58)

Sunshine Carrot Salad (page 58)

Cranberry-Pear Conserve (page 59)

Festive Noodle Pudding (page 60)

Ruby Borscht

1. Combine the beets, carrots, onion, celery, broth or water, brown sugar, bouillon granules, and pepper in a 4-quart pot, and bring to a boil over high heat. Reduce the heat to low, cover, and simmer for 20 minutes, or until the vegetables are tender.

2. Add the cabbage, and simmer uncovered for 15 minutes, or until the cabbage is tender. Remove the pot from the heat and stir in the vinegar.

3. Ladle the soup into individual serving bowls. Top each serving with a rounded tablespoon of sour cream and a sprinkling of dill, and serve.

Yield: 12 servings

4 cups coarsely shredded peeled beets (about 1¼ pounds)

2 cups diced peeled carrots (about 2 large)

1½ cups chopped onion

1 cup thinly sliced celery

7 cups unsalted beef broth or water

3–4 tablespoons brown sugar

1 tablespoon beef bouillon granules

¼ teaspoon coarsely ground black pepper

2 cups thinly sliced cabbage

¼ cup white wine vinegar

TOPPINGS

1½ cups nonfat sour cream

2 tablespoons minced fresh dill

NUTRITIONAL FACTS (PER 1-CUP SERVING)

Calories: 67	Fat: 0.4 g	Protein: 2.6 g
Cholesterol: 0 mg	Fiber: 2.3 g	Sodium: 335 mg

Chunky Applesauce

1. Peel the apples, and cut them into ½-inch chunks. Place the apple chunks and juice concentrate in a 3-quart pot, and stir to combine. Cover and cook over medium-low heat, stirring occasionally, for about 30 minutes, or until the apples are soft.

2. Using a potato masher, mash the mixture to the desired consistency. Serve warm or cold, sprinkling the sauce with a little cinnamon if desired.

Yield: 12 servings

4 pounds Granny Smith apples (14 to 16 medium)

½ cup frozen apple juice concentrate, thawed

Ground cinnamon (optional)

NUTRITIONAL FACTS (PER ⅓-CUP SERVING)

Calories: 78	Fiber: 2.0 g
Cholesterol: 0 mg	Protein: 0.2 g
Fat: 0.3 g	Sodium: 2 mg

Roast Turkey Breast
With Sourdough Stuffing

Yield: 12 servings

7-pound turkey breast (with bones)

SOURDOUGH STUFFING

1-pound loaf sourdough bread

1¼ cups finely chopped onion

1 cup finely chopped celery

1 cup chopped fresh mushrooms

1¼ teaspoons poultry seasoning

1¼ teaspoons dried savory

¼ teaspoon ground black pepper

4 egg whites

1¼ cups chicken broth

NUTRITIONAL FACTS
(PER 3 OUNCES MEAT
PLUS ⅔ CUP STUFFING)

Calories: 278	Fiber: 1.6 g
Chol.: 97 mg	Protein: 39 g
Fat: 2.5 g	Sodium: 337 mg

Your butcher can debone the turkey breast for you, or you can debone the breast yourself by following the instructions provided below.

1. To debone the turkey breast, place the breast, skin side down, on a large cutting board. Use a small sharp knife to cut along the bones, starting at the ribs, to release the meat. As you cut around the wishbone and backbone, be careful not to cut through the skin. Discard the bones, and lay the meat flat, skin side down. You should now have a butterfly-shaped piece of meat that is approximately 10 by 14 inches in size. Trim away any jagged edges, rinse with cool water, and pat dry. (Debone the breast up to 24 hours in advance, if desired, and refrigerate the meat until you're ready to fully prepare the dish.)

2. To make the stuffing, tear ¾ of the bread into small pieces. Place the pieces in a food processor or blender, and process into coarse crumbs. Measure the crumbs. There should be 6 cups. (Adjust the amount if necessary.) Cut the remaining bread into ½-inch cubes, and measure the cubes(6 cups). (Adjust the amount if necessary.)

3. Place the bread crumbs and cubes in a large bowl, and add the onion, celery, mushrooms, seasonings, and egg whites. Toss to mix well.

4. Set aside 3 cups of stuffing to stuff the turkey breast. Add ¼ cup of chicken broth to the remaining stuffing, and toss to mix well. Coat a 2-quart casserole dish with nonstick cooking spray, and place the stuffing in the dish. Bake uncovered at 325°F for 1 hour, or until lightly browned on top. (Place the casserole in the oven 1 hour before the turkey is done.)

5. To stuff the turkey breast, lay breast flat, skin side down, on a clean surface, and spread the 3 cups of reserved stuffing over half the breast, spread the stuffing from the center all the way to outer edges. Fold other breast half over stuffing to cover, use a heavy string to tie breast together in 3 places.

6. Place the breast on a rack in a large roasting pan, and pour the remaining cup of chicken broth into the pan. Cover the pan loosely with aluminum foil, and bake at 325°F for 1 hour and 10 minutes. Uncover the pan, and bake for 30 additional minutes, or until the skin is golden brown and a meat thermometer inserted in the breast registers 170°F. Occasionally baste with the pan juices during cooking. (Note that the juices which remain in the pan will be used to make Savory Gravy.)

7. Transfer the turkey breast to a serving platter. Cover the turkey loosely with aluminum foil, and let sit for 15 minutes before slicing. Serve with Savory Gravy.

Savory Gravy

1. Combine the flour and milk in a jar with a tight-fitting lid, and shake until smooth. Set aside.

2. Pour the turkey drippings from the roast turkey breast into a fat separator cup. (If you don't have a separator cup, pour the drippings into a bowl, add a few ice cubes, and skim off the fat once it rises and hardens.) Pour the fat-free drippings into a 2-cup measure, and add enough water to bring the volume up to 1¾ cups.

3. Pour the drippings mixture into a 1½-quart saucepan, and add the bouillon granules and seasonings. Bring the mixture to a boil over medium heat, reduce the heat to low, and simmer for 5 minutes.

4. Slowly stir the flour mixture into the gravy, and continue to cook and stir until the mixture is thickened and bubbly. Transfer the gravy to a warmed gravy boat or pitcher, and serve hot with the stuffed turkey breast.

Yield: 2¼ cups

¼ cup plus 1½ teaspoons unbleached flour

½ cup skim milk

Roast turkey drippings

1 teaspoon chicken bouillon granules

¼ teaspoon poultry seasoning

¼ teaspoon dried savory

⅛ teaspoon ground black pepper

NUTRITIONAL FACTS (PER TABLESPOON)

Calories: 7	Fat: 0 g	Protein: 0.4 g
Cholesterol: 0 mg	Fiber: 0 g	Sodium: 30 mg

Green Beans and Mushrooms

Yield: 12 servings

2 pounds fresh green beans

2 cups sliced fresh mushrooms

¼ cup water

1½ teaspoons chicken bouillon granules

1 teaspoon dried thyme

¼ teaspoon ground black pepper

1. Rinse the beans with cool water. Trim the ends, and cut into 1-inch pieces. Place the beans and the remaining ingredients in a 3-quart pot, and stir to mix well.

2. Bring the beans to a boil over medium heat. Reduce the heat to low, cover, and, stirring occasionally, simmer for 12 to 15 minutes, or until the beans are just tender. (Add a tablespoon or 2 of water if the pot becomes too dry.) Serve immediately.

Time-Saving Tip

To make this dish totally fuss-free, substitute 2 pounds of frozen (thawed) cut green beans for the fresh green beans.

NUTRITIONAL FACTS (PER ½-CUP SERVING)

Calories: 29	Fat: 0.2 g	Protein: 1.7 g
Cholesterol: 0 mg	Fiber: 2.7 g	Sodium: 132 mg

Sunshine Carrot Salad

Yield: 12 servings

4 cups grated carrots (about 8 medium-large)

1 can (20 ounces) pineapple chunks in juice, drained, or 2 cups fresh pineapple chunks

2 cans (11 ounces each) mandarin orange sections in juice or light syrup, drained

1 cup golden raisins

DRESSING

¾ cup nonfat sour cream

½ cup nonfat or reduced-fat mayonnaise

1. Combine the carrots, pineapple chunks, oranges, and raisins in a large bowl, and toss gently to mix. Combine the dressing ingredients in a small bowl, and spread over the carrot mixture. Toss gently to mix well.

2. Cover the salad and chill for at least 2 hours before serving.

NUTRITIONAL FACTS (PER ½-CUP SERVING)

Calories: 106	Fat: 0.3 g	Protein: 2.2 g
Cholesterol: 0 mg	Fiber: 2 g	Sodium: 139 mg

Cranberry-Pear Conserve

1. Combine all of the ingredients in a 2-quart pot, and bring to a boil over medium-high heat. Reduce the heat to low, and simmer uncovered, stirring occasionally, for about 10 minutes, or until the cranberry skins have popped open and the mixture has thickened.

2. Cover the conserve and chill for several hours or overnight. Serve as an accompaniment to the turkey.

Yield: 12 servings

3 cups diced fresh pears (about 3 medium)

2 cups fresh or frozen cranberries, stemmed

¾ cup pear nectar

¼ cup light brown sugar

¼ cup golden raisins

¼ teaspoon ground cinnamon

¼ teaspoon ground nutmeg

¼ teaspoon ground ginger

NUTRITIONAL FACTS (PER ¼-CUP SERVING)

Calories: 60	Fat: 0.2 g	Protein: 0.4 g
Cholesterol: 0 mg	Fiber: 1.7 g	Sodium: 2 mg

Potato Latkes

1. Scrub the potatoes, but leave them unpeeled. Coarsely grate the potatoes into a large bowl of ice water. Let sit for 5 minutes. Drain off the water, and roll the grated potatoes in a clean kitchen towel to remove excess water. Coarsely grate the onions.

2. Place the grated potatoes and onions in a large bowl, and add the remaining ingredients. Stir to mix well.

3. Coat a large nonstick skillet or griddle with nonstick cooking spray, and place it over medium-high heat. For each pancake, spoon ¼ cup of the batter onto the skillet, and spread to form a 3½-inch pancake. Cook for 6 minutes on each side over medium-low heat, or until golden brown on the outside and tender on the inside. As the pancakes are done, transfer them to a serving plate and keep warm in a preheated oven.

4. Serve warm with Chunky Applesauce or nonfat sour cream.

Yield: 24 pancakes

2½ pounds large baking potatoes

1 medium Spanish onion

4 egg whites

2 tablespoons unbleached flour

½ teaspoon salt

¼ teaspoon ground white pepper

NUTRITIONAL FACTS (PER PANCAKE)

Calories: 50	Fiber: 1.1 g
Cholesterol: 0 mg	Protein: 1.1 g
Fat: 0 g	Sodium: 48 mg

Festive Noodle Pudding

Yield: 12 servings

8 ounces medium or wide eggless noodles

2 cups dry curd or nonfat cottage cheese

1 cup nonfat or reduced-fat cream cheese, softened to room temperature

1½ cups fat-free egg substitute

½ cup sugar

2 teaspoons vanilla extract

2 cups chopped apples (about 3 medium)

½ cup plus 2 tablespoons coarsely chopped fresh or frozen cranberries, stemmed

½ cup golden raisins

TOPPING

3 tablespoons sugar

2 tablespoons chopped walnuts

1. Cook the noodles al dente according to package directions. Drain, rinse with cool water, and drain again. Set aside.

2. Combine the cottage cheese, cream cheese, egg substitute, sugar, and vanilla extract in a large bowl, and stir to mix well. Add the drained noodles, apples, cranberries, and raisins, and toss gently to mix.

3. Coat an 8-x-12-inch pan with nonstick cooking spray, and spread the noodle mixture evenly in the pan. Combine the topping ingredients in a small bowl, and sprinkle over the noodle mixture.

4. Bake uncovered at 350°F for about 1 hour and 10 minutes, or until a sharp knife inserted halfway between the edge of the pan and the center comes out clean. Cool for 20 minutes, cut into squares, and serve warm or at room temperature.

NUTRITIONAL FACTS (PER SERVING)

Calories: 210	Fat: 1.2 g	Protein: 13 g
Cholesterol: 5 mg	Fiber: 1.3 g	Sodium: 145 mg

Variation

For variety, omit the apples and instead use 2 cups of frozen pitted sweet cherries, cut in half, or 2 cups of drained pineapple tidbits.

Passover

Matzo----a cracker-like unleavened bread----takes center stage during the week of Passover. Fortunately, matzo has always been fat-free, and is wonderfully versatile as well. In the Seder menu presented in this section, you'll find this and other traditional Passover foods married with healthful fat-free ingredients to make untraditionally light and delicious holiday dishes.

Our Passover menu offers another collection of crowd-pleasing dishes, many of which are Passover favorites given fat-free makeovers for a healthy and satisfying holiday dinner.

Our menu begins with a Passover must---- matzo ball soup. This version features a tasty broth enriched with sweet potatoes, as well as matzo balls made light and tender with whipped egg whites instead of egg yolks and oil.

The soup course is followed by a hearty main dish----Braised Beef with Carrots and Prunes. Beef round replaces the traditional brisket in this recipe to cut the fat by almost 75 percent. On the side are Asparagus Vinaigrette, a simple but savory dish, and flavorful Scalloped Tomato Matzo. For dessert, enjoy warm Apple Matzo Kugel. Moistened with fresh apples and apple juice instead of butter or margarine, this dessert is bursting with flavor.

To save time on the day of your dinner, much of this meal can be made ahead, while the rest can be easily assembled during the hours before your guests arrive. Golden Matzo Soup, for instance, can be prepared the day before your dinner. Cover the soup and chill it, and reheat just before serving.

The entrée of braised beef can be easily assembled in the hours before guests arrive, and then placed in the oven, where it will require little attention until it's time to make the gravy. Or, if you choose, make this dish the day before your dinner, and reheat it right before serving.

Scalloped Tomato Matzo, one of the menu's two accompaniments, must be assembled and baked directly before serving time. But if you slice the onions and assemble the ingredients in advance, this dish can be whipped together in a matter of minutes.

Asparagus Vinaigrette is the perfect make-ahead dish, as it should be fully prepared the day before your Seder to allow the flavors to blend. Arrange these flavorful vegetables in a serving bowl, and chill until dinner begins.

Our Seder's dessert can be made the day before your dinner, if desired, and refrigerated until an hour before serving. Cover it with aluminum foil and reheat it for fifteen to twenty minutes if you'd like to serve it warm. For even less fuss, serve it at room temperature. It will be equally delicious!

Passover Seder

Menu

SERVES 6 TO 8

Golden Matzo Ball Soup (page 63)

*Braised Beef
With Carrots and Prunes* (page 64)

Asparagus Vinaigrette (page 65)

Scalloped Tomato Matzo (page 65)

Apple Matzo Kugel (page 66)

Fluffy Fat-Free Matzo Balls

1. Place the egg whites in the bowl of an electric mixer, and sprinkle with the salt. Beat at high speed until stiff peaks form when the beaters are removed. Remove the beaters, and gently fold in the matzo meal, 3 tablespoons at a time. Cover the mixture, and chill for 15 minutes.

2. Half fill a 6-quart stock pot with water, and bring to a rapid boil over high heat. Add the chicken bouillon granules or salt if desired. Coat your hands with nonstick cooking spray, and gently shape the chilled matzo meal mixture into 16 (1¼-inch) balls. Drop the balls into the boiling water (or unsalted chicken or vegetable stock instead of water), reduce the heat to medium-low, and cover the pot. Simmer for 20 minutes, or until the matzo balls are firm.

3. Remove the matzo balls with a slotted spoon, and add immediately to your chicken soup, or store in a covered container for 1 to 2 days.

Yield: 8 servings

6 egg whites, warmed to room temperature

½ teaspoon salt

1 cup plus 2 tablespoons matzo meal

1 teaspoon chicken bouillon granules, or ½ teaspoon salt (optional)

NUTRITIONAL FACTS (PER SERVING)

Calories: 48   Fiber: 0.3 g
Cholesterol: 0 mg Protein: 3.6 g
Fat:

Golden Matzo Ball Soup

1. Place the chicken stock, sweet potato or squash, onion, celery, and bouillon in a 2½-quart pot. Bring to a boil over high heat. Then reduce the heat to low and cover the pot. Simmer for 30 minutes, or until the vegetables are very tender.

2. Use a slotted spoon to transfer the vegetables from the pot to a blender or food processor. Add 1 cup of the hot broth, and process, with the lid slightly ajar, for 30 seconds, or until the mixture is smooth. Return the blended mixture to the pot.

3. Add the matzo balls to the soup, and simmer, covered, for 10 minutes. Ladle the soup into individual serving bowls, placing 2 matzo balls in each bowl, and serve hot.

Yield: 8 servings

5 cups unsalted vegetable or chicken stock

1¼ cups peeled and diced sweet potato or butternut squash

1 medium yellow onion, chopped

1 stalk celery, thinly sliced

2 teaspoons vegetable or chicken bouillon granules

NUTRITIONAL FACTS (PER SERVING)

Calories: 48   Fiber: 0.3 g
Cholesterol: 0 mg Protein: 3.6 g
Fat:

Braised Beef With Carrots and Prunes

Yield: 8 servings

2½-lb. top round roast or London broil

½ teaspoon coarsely ground pepper

1 medium yellow onion, chopped

½ cup beef broth

6 large carrots (about 1¼ pounds), peeled and cut into ¼-inch slices

1 cup pitted prunes

½ teaspoon ground cinnamon

½ teaspoon salt

1 tablespoon lemon juice

3 tablespoons brown sugar

1. Trim any visible fat from the meat. Rinse the meat, and pat it dry with paper towels. Sprinkle both sides with pepper.

2. Coat a large cast-iron skillet or Dutch oven with nonstick cooking spray, and preheat over medium-high heat. Place the meat in the skillet, and brown it for 2 minutes on each side. Remove the skillet from the heat, and spread the onions on the meat. Pour the beef broth in the bottom of the skillet, cover the skillet tightly, and bake at 325°F for 2 hours.

3. Remove the skillet from the oven, and carefully remove the cover. (Steam will escape.) Place the carrots and prunes around the meat, and sprinkle the meat, carrots, and prunes with the cinnamon, salt, and lemon juice. Cover the skillet tightly, and return it to the oven for another 30 minutes, or until the meatand carrots are tender. Transfer the meat, carrots, and prunes to a serving platter, and keep warm.

4. To make the gravy, pour the meat drippings into a fat separator cup. (If you don't have a separator cup, pour the drippings into a bowl, add a few ice cubes, and skim off the fat once it rises and hardens.) Pour the fat-free drippings into a 1-cup measure, and add enough water to bring the volume up to ¾ cup.

5. Return the drippings mixture to the skillet, and add the brown sugar. Bring the mixture to a boil over medium heat, and cook and stir for 1 minute, or until the sugar is dissolved. Transfer the gravy to a warmed gravy boat or pitcher, and serve hot with the meat and vegetables.

NUTRITIONAL FACTS (PER SERVING)

Calories: 283	Fat: 4.6 g	Protein: 28 g
Cholesterol: 59 mg	Fiber: 5.1 g	Sodium: 344 mg

Asparagus Vinaigrette

Yield: 8 servings

1. Combine the vegetables in a shallow dish. Combine the dressing ingredients in a small bowl until the sugar dissolves, and pour over the vegetables. Toss to mix well.

2. Cover the salad and chill for several hours or overnight before serving.

2 packages (10 ounces each) frozen cut asparagus, thawed, or 4 cups 1-inch asparagus pieces, steamed

¼ cup finely chopped onion

½ cup diced red bell pepper

DRESSING

2 tablespoons white wine vinegar

2 tablespoons lemon juice

1 tablespoon grainy Dijon mustard

1 tablespoon olive oil (optional)

¾ teaspoon dried oregano

1 tablespoon sugar

¼ teaspoon salt

NUTRITIONAL FACTS (PER ½-CUP SERVING)

Calories: 30	Fat: 0.3 g	Protein: 2.2 g
Cholesterol: 0 mg	Fiber: 1.6 g	Sodium: 89 mg

Scalloped Tomato Matzo

Yield: 8 servings

1. In a large bowl, combine the tomatoes, salt, and pepper.

2. Coat an 8-inch square pan with cooking spray. Cover the bottom of the pan with half of the onions. Lay 1 matzo over the onions, and top with half of the tomatoes. Place another matzo over the tomatoes, and cover with the remaining tomatoes. Crumble the remaining matzo into small pieces, and sprinkle over the top. Separate the remaining onion into rings, and arrange over the matzo.

3. Bake uncovered at 350°F for 40 minutes, or until the tomatoes are bubbly and the onion rings are browned. Serve hot.

2 cans (1 pound each) unsalted stewed tomatoes, undrained

½ teaspoon salt

¼ teaspoon ground black pepper

1 large Spanish onion, thinly sliced

3 matzos

NUTRITIONAL FACTS (PER ¾-CUP SERVING)

Calories: 81	Fat: 0.3 g	Protein: 2 g
Cholesterol: 0 mg	Fiber: 2.5 g	Sodium: 152 mg

Apple Matzo Kugel

Yield: 9 servings

2 cups matzo farfel, or 3½ matzos, broken into small pieces

1 cup apple juice

1 cup fat-free egg substitute

¼ cup plus 2 tablespoons sugar

½ teaspoon ground cinnamon

¼ teaspoon salt

2½ cups finely chopped tart apples (about 4 medium)

½ cup golden raisins

¼ cup chopped walnuts (optional)

TOPPING

1 tablespoon plus 1 teaspoon finely ground walnuts

1 tablespoon plus 1 teaspoon sugar

1. Combine topping ingredients in a small bowl, and set aside.

2. Place the matzo farfel in a large bowl. Add the apple juice, and stir to mix well. Set aside for 5 minutes.

3. Add the egg substitute, sugar, cinnamon, and salt to the matzo mixture, and stir gently to mix well. Stir in the apples and raisins and, if desired, the walnuts.

4. Coat an 8-inch square pan with nonstick cooking spray, and spread the mixture evenly in the pan. Sprinkle with the topping, and bake at 350°F for 40 minutes, or until a sharp knife inserted in the center comes out clean. Let sit for 15 minutes before cutting into squares. Serve warm or at room temperature.

NUTRITIONAL FACTS (PER ⅔-CUP SERVING)

Calories: 184	Fat: 1 g	Protein: 5.1 g
Cholesterol: 0 mg	Fiber: 1.9 g	Sodium: 110 mg

Passover Seder, A Time of Remembrance
Top Left: Asparagus Vinaigrette (page 65)
Top Right: Golden Matzo Ball Soup (page 63)
Bottom: Braised Beef With Carrots and Prunes (page 64)

A Glorious Easter Dinner
Top Left: Company Carrot-Raisin Salad (page 70)
Top Right: Fresh-Steamed Asparagus With Honey Mustard Sauce (page 71)
Bottom: Rosemary Roasted Tenderloin (page 69)

A Hearty New Year's Day Dinner
Top: Moist Cornmeal Muffins (page 81)
Center Left: Country-Style Cabbage (page 80)
Center Right: Cinnamon Apples (page 80)
Bottom: Braised Beef Round With Potatoes and Carrots (page 79)

A Romantic Valentine's Dinner
Top: Spinach and Mushroom Salad (page 85)
Bottom Left: Lemon Scallops Linguine (page 86)
Bottom Right: Dilled Carrots (page 88)

A Haunting Halloween Buffet
Top Left: Hot Apple Cider (page 93)
Top Right: Mini Mexican Corn Muffins (page 96)
Center Left: Two-Bean Chili (page 95)
Center Right: Black Olive Dip (page 97)

A Sumptuous Selection of Sinless Desserts
Top: Fresh Fruit Trifle (page 114)
Bottom Left: Cranberry Upside-Down Cake (page 112)
Bottom Right: Chocolate-Almond Cannoli Cake (page 113)

Easter

Looking for an alternative to that traditional salty Easter ham and all the fatty trimmings? In this section, you'll find a delightful but simple and elegant Easter dinner.

Simple, yet special enough for any occasion, this menu captures the essence of spring with its fresh, light, and flavorful dishes.

Creamy Cucumber Dip served with fresh vegetables and whole grain crackers makes for a great beginning. Then comes a marinated tenderloin of pork, fragrant with rosemary and garlic. Corn Pudding, the perfect accompaniment, is made thick and rich with puréed corn instead of cream. Company Carrot-Raisin Salad and Fresh-Steamed Asparagus with a warm Honey Mustard Sauce add balance and color while continuing the spring theme. And the crowning touch? Stunning Chocolate Raspberry Torte. Rich, chocolatey, and moist, this delightful dessert is amazingly simple to make. And your guests won't believe it's fat-free!

Most of the preparations for this dinner can be made well ahead of time, leaving you free to enjoy Easter Sunday with your guests. The day before the dinner, prepare the Creamy Cucumber Dip, and cut up the raw vegetables that will accompany it. The vegetables will stay fresh and crisp if kept chilled in plastic bags or airtight containers.

Place the pork tenderloin in the marinade the day before so that it will be ready to roast an hour or so before your dinner. At the same time, prepare the Creamy Corn Pudding to the point of baking, and store it in a covered container in the refrigerator. When ready to bake, transfer the pudding to a casserole dish. Once the roast and pudding are in the oven, they will require little attention.

The Company Carrot-Raisin Salad can be prepared as early as a day in advance, as can the sauce for the asparagus. Last-minute preparations for the asparagus should take only minutes of your time.

The cakes for the Chocolate Raspberry Torte can also be baked the day before your dinner. Then assemble the dessert a few hours before your guests arrive, and chill it until serving time. Only you will know how easy it was to prepare this elegant and impressive dessert!

Easter Dinner

SERVES 8 TO 10

Creamy Cucumber Dip (page 26)
With Fresh Vegetables and Crackers

Rosemary Roasted Tenderloin (page 69)

Creamy Corn Pudding (page 70)

Company Carrot-Raisin Salad (page 70)

Fresh-Steamed Asparagus
With Honey Mustard Sauce (page 71)

Chocolate Raspberry Torte (page 72)

Rosemary Roasted Tenderloin

1. Trim the tenderloins of any visible fat and membranes. Rinse with cool water, and pat dry with paper towels. Place the tenderloins in a shallow nonmetal dish.

2. In a small bowl, combine the marinade ingredients. Pour the marinade over the meat, turning the tenderloins to coat all sides. Cover and refrigerate for several hours or overnight.

3. When ready to bake, coat a 13-x-16-inch roasting pan with nonstick cooking spray and place the tenderloins in the pan, spacing them at least 2 inches apart. Pour any remaining marinade over the tenderloins, and bake at 350°F for about 45 minutes, or until an instant-read thermometer inserted in the center of a tenderloin registers 160°F and the meat is no longer pink inside.

4. Remove the pan from the oven, cover loosely with aluminum foil, and let sit for 5 minutes before slicing thinly at an angle. Serve immediately.

Yield: 12 servings

3 pork tenderloins, 1 pound each

MARINADE

¼ cup plus 1 tablespoon frozen apple juice concentrate, thawed

2 tablespoons plus 1½ teaspoons Dijon mustard

2 tablespoons plus 1½ teaspoons fresh rosemary leaves, or 2½ teaspoons dried

5 cloves garlic, crushed

½ teaspoon coarsely ground black pepper

NUTRITIONAL FACTS (PER 3-OUNCE SERVING)

Calories: 144	Fat: 4.2 g	Protein: 24.6 g
Cholesterol: 79 mg	Fiber: 0 g	Sodium: 76 mg

Creamy Corn Pudding

Yield: 10 servings

4½ cups fresh or frozen (thawed) whole kernel corn

½ cup chopped onion

1½ cups skim milk

¾ cup fat-free egg substitute

3 tablespoons unbleached flour

¼ teaspoon ground white pepper

¼ teaspoon ground nutmeg

½ teaspoon salt

1. Place 1½ cups of the corn and all of the remaining ingredients in a blender or food processor. Process for 1 minute, or until the mixture is smooth. Place the processed mixture in a large bowl, add the remaining corn kernels, and stir to mix well.

2. Coat a 2½-quart casserole dish with nonstick cooking spray, and pour the corn mixture into the dish. Bake at 350°F for 1 hour and 15 minutes, or until a sharp knife inserted midway between the center of the dish and the rim comes out clean. Remove the dish from the oven, and let sit for 10 minutes before serving.

NUTRITIONAL FACTS (PER ½-CUP SERVING)

Calories: 84	Fat: 0.8 g	Protein: 3.9 g
Cholesterol: 0 mg	Fiber: 2.1 g	Sodium: 136 mg

Company Carrot-Raisin Salad

Yield: 10 servings

5 cups grated carrots (about 2 pounds)

¾ cup thinly sliced celery

⅔ cup dark raisins

DRESSING

⅓ cup nonfat or reduced-fat mayonnaise

¼ cup frozen apple juice concentrate, thawed

1. Combine the carrots, celery, and raisins in a large bowl, and toss to mix well. Combine the dressing ingredients in a small bowl, and pour over the carrot mixture. Toss to mix well.

2. Cover the salad and chill for several hours or overnight before serving.

NUTRITIONAL FACTS (PER ½-CUP SERVING)

Calories: 83	Fat: 0.2 g	Protein: 1.2 g
Cholesterol: 0 mg	Fiber: 2.4 g	Sodium: 126 mg

Fresh-Steamed Asparagus With Honey Mustard Sauce

Yield: 10 servings

2½ pounds fresh asparagus spears

HONEY MUSTARD SAUCE

2 tablespoons honey

2 tablespoons Dijon mustard

2 tablespoons lemon juice

¼ cup nonfat or reduced-fat mayonnaise

1. Combine the sauce ingredients in a small saucepan, and stir until smooth. Set aside.

2. Rinse the asparagus with cool running water, and snap off the tough stem ends. Arrange the asparagus spears in a microwave or conventional steamer. Cover and cook at high power or over medium-high heat for 4 to 6 minutes, or just until the spears are crisp-tender. Transfer the asparagus to a serving dish.

3. While the asparagus are cooking, place the sauce over medium heat, and cook, stirring constantly, just until the sauce is heated through. Drizzle the sauce over the asparagus, and serve immediately.

NUTRITIONAL FACTS (PER SERVING)

Calories: 44	Fat: 0.3 g	Protein: 2.5 g
Cholesterol: 0 mg	Fiber: 2.3 g	Sodium: 109 mg

Chocolate Raspberry Torte

Yield: 16 servings

1½ cups unbleached flour

1 cup oat flour

1½ cups sugar

½ cup cocoa powder

2 teaspoons baking soda

1 cup coffee, cooled to room
   temperature, or 1 cup water

1½ cups skim milk

2 teaspoons vanilla extract

¾ cup raspberry jam or fruit spread

FROSTING

1¼ cups light whipped topping

⅓ cup nonfat raspberry yogurt

1. In a large bowl, combine the flours, sugar, cocoa, and baking soda, and stir to mix well. Add the coffee or water and the milk and vanilla extract, and mix with a wire whisk until the batter is smooth. (The batter will be thin.)

2. Coat four 8-inch round pans with nonstick cooking spray. Divide the batter among the pans, and bake at 350°F for 18 to 20 minutes, or just until the top springs back when lightly touched and a wooden toothpick inserted in the center comes out clean. Be careful not to overbake. Let the cakes cool to room temperature in the pans.

3. Invert 1 cake onto a serving platter, and spread with ¼ cup of the jam. Add the next two layers, spreading each with jam. Top with the final layer.

4. Place the whipped topping in a small bowl, and gently fold the yogurt into the topping. Spread the frosting over the sides and top of the cake. Chill the cake for several hours, cut into wedges, and serve.

NUTRITIONAL FACTS (PER SERVING)

| Calories: 210 | Fat: 1.8 g | Protein: 3.7 g |
| Cholesterol: 0 mg | Fiber: 2 g | Sodium: 136 mg |

Part Three

Celebrations and Parties

Each calendar year is studded with special days that invite us to share in celebrations ranging from Halloween costume party to a New Year's Celebration. For most of us, each of these days provides a welcome time of relaxation and festive events. Perhaps most important, each is a wonderful reason to get together with family and friends.

Over the years, the uniqueness of each holiday has come to be reflected by certain types of food and gatherings. With today's emphasis on healthy, low-fat eating, though, many people are now looking for new menu ideas that provide good nutrition without sacrificing good taste. The remainder of Part Three will fill the bill by presenting festive menus that will delight your guests with great-tasting, satisfying fare that is also high in nutrition.

The calendar year begins with a New Year's Day menu featuring Hoppin' John----a traditional good-luck dish that's served over brown rice for hearty eating. For those who prefer a meat entrée, Braised Beef Round With Potatoes and Carrots is a delicious alternative. Rounding out the meal is Country-Style Cabbage, spicy Cinnamon Apples, savory Cornmeal Muffins, and a super-moist Fat-Free Carrot Cake With Creamy Cheese Frosting.

Valentine's Day brings a romantic and elegant dinner for two. After an appetizer of Spiced Artichoke Spread, treat your special someone to a light Spinach and Mushroom Salad followed by either Lemon Scallops Linguine or Glazed Turkey Cutlets With Rice. Dilled Carrots are the perfect accompaniment to either entrée. For dessert, choose between Poached Pears, turned an appropriate red with Warm Raspberry Sauce, and creamy Tiramisu for Two.

Finally, there's a hearty Halloween buffet that's sure to delight trick-or-treaters and parents alike. Hot Apple Cider provides much-needed warmth on a chilly fall evening, while Fiesta Quesadillas, Two-Bean Chili, and Mini Mexican Corn Muffins satisfy even the hungriest ghosts and goblins. What's for dessert? Black Magic Cake, of course.

As you use one of the following menus to plan a party or get-together, feel free to borrow recipes from other menus or from other sections of the book. For instance, if the menu you've chosen includes an appetizer that you feel wouldn't appeal to your family, just look in

Part One, which gives recipes for dozens of delightful appetizers. Or perhaps the menu includes a dessert that requires last-minute attention, but you are planning a no-fuss picnic lunch. Turn to Part Four, where you'll be sure to find a dessert that's both delicious and portable.

So fire up the grill----or build a fire in the fireplace----and invite your friends over for a special-occasion meal that's low on fat and high on taste. With these easy-to-follow recipes and easy-serving menus, your next get-together is sure to be one that will not only please your guests, but will leave you time to enjoy the festivities, too.

New Year's Day

Resolving to eat more healthfully is probably *the* most common New Year's resolution. Fortunately, this hearty winter's meal is just what the doctor ordered.

While dinner finishes cooking, stave off hunger with Broccoli Cheese Dip. For an attractive presentation, remove three or four large outer leaves from a head of cabbage, and use them to form a bowl for the dip. Then place the dip in the center of a platter, and surround it with raw vegetables and whole grain crackers.

The traditional New Year's Day meal of Hoppin' John----minus the ham hocks----takes center stage as a high-nutrient, low-fat entrée. Rich in protein, vitamins, and minerals, beans are the perfect fat-free alternative to meat. As a bonus, beans are loaded with complex carbohydrates and cholesterol-lowering soluble fiber.

If Hoppin' John is not your pleasure, try Braised Beef Round With Potatoes and Carrots. Made with the leanest beef available, this stick-to-your-ribs dish is sure to delight your family's meat-and-potato lovers.

Country-Style Cabbage, Cinnamon Apples, and Moist Cornmeal Muffins round out this simple yet satisfying meal. Last but not least is luscious Fat-Free Carrot Cake. Moistened with fruit juice instead of the usual oil and topped with a creamy fat-free frosting, this is certain to become a family favorite.

A little advance planning makes this meal a breeze. The day before the party, make the Broccoli Cheese Dip and cut up the raw vegetables. Then keep the vegetables crisp by storing them in airtight plastic containers.

Hoppin' John, too, can be prepared the day before the party, and then reheated just before serving. If you've chosen to make the Braised Beef, start preparing it about two and a half hours before serving. This delicious dish requires little attention as it bakes.

Moist Cornmeal Muffins and Fat-Free Carrot Cake can also be baked a day in advance. Just before serving, reheat the muffins in a microwave or conventional oven to bring out that fresh-baked flavor. The carrot cake, of course, must be refrigerated until you're ready to bring it out to rave reviews.

New Year's Dinner

SERVES 6 TO 8

Broccoli Cheese Dip (page 27)
With Raw Vegetables and Crackers

Hoppin' John (page 75) with Brown Rice (page 77)
or Braised Beef Round With Potatoes and Carrots (page 79)

Country-Style Cabbage (page 80)

Cinnamon Apples (page 80)

Moist Cornmeal Muffins (page 80)

Fat-Free Carrot Cake
With Creamy Cheese Frosting (page 82)

Hoppin' John

This hearty dish is a New Year's tradition in the South, where it is believed to bring good luck when eaten on New Year's Day.

1. Place the black-eyed peas in a 4-quart pot, and add 2½ quarts of water. Cover and soak for 4 hours or overnight. (Place the pot in the refrigerator if soaking for more than 4 hours.) When you are ready to cook, drain off the soaking water and return the peas to the pot.

2. Add all of the remaining ingredients, except for the toppings, to the pot, and bring the mixture to a boil over high heat. Lower the heat, and cover and simmer for 45 minutes to an hour, or until the beans are tender and the liquid has thickened. Stir occasionally, and add more water if needed. (The liquid should barely cover the peas.)

3. Serve hot over brown rice, garnishing each serving with 1 tablespoon each of tomatoes and scallions, if desired. Pass the Tabasco sauce if your family and friends like it hot!

Yield: 9 servings

3 cups dried black-eyed peas, sorted

4 cups water or unsalted chicken stock

1 medium yellow onion, chopped

1½ teaspoons crushed fresh garlic

1½ teaspoons dried sage

2 teaspoons chicken or vegetable bouillon granules, or 8 ounces lean ham, diced

¼ teaspoon ground black pepper

¼ teaspoon ground cayenne pepper

TOPPINGS

1 cup finely chopped tomatoes (optional)

1 cup finely chopped scallions (optional)

Tabasco pepper sauce (optional)

NUTRITIONAL FACTS (PER 1-CUP SERVING)

Calories: 195	Fat: 0.7 g	Protein: 13 g
Cholesterol: 0 mg	Fiber: 4.6 g	Sodium: 187 mg

Brown Rice

Rinsing the rice before cooking is not absolutely necessary, but does make the rice fluffier. This recipe will guide you in making delicious brown rice on your stove top. For instructions on making the fluffiest rice imaginable in a rice cooker, see the inset on page 78.

1. Place the rice in a strainer, and rinse under running water.

2. Place the rice and the vegetable stock or water in a 2½-quart pot, and bring to a boil over high heat. Reduce the heat to low, stir the rice, and cover.

Yield: 8 servings

2 cups uncooked long grain brown rice

4½ cups unsalted vegetable stock or water

3. Allow the rice to simmer, covered, for 50 minutes, or until the rice is tender and the liquid has been absorbed. Do not stir the rice while it is cooking, as this can result in sticky rice.

4. Remove the rice from the heat, and let sit, covered, for 5 minutes. Fluff with a fork, and serve hot.

NUTRITIONAL FACTS (PER ¾-CUP SERVING)

Calories: 162	Fat: 1.2 g	Protein: 3.7 g
Cholesterol: 0 mg	Fiber: 2.6 g	Sodium: 7 mg

Using a Rice Cooker

A rice cooker, which is available in most department stores, makes it a snap to cook dry, fluffy rice----even when brown rice is on the menu. As a bonus, most rice cookers act as warmers to keep the prepared rice at the right temperature until serving time. The following simple directions will give you perfect brown rice each and every time you make it.

Perfect Brown Rice

Yield: 12 servings

2 cups uncooked long grain brown rice

5 cups unsalted vegetable stock or water

1. Place the rice in a strainer, and rinse under running water.

2. Place the rice and the vegetable stock or water in a 2-quart or larger rice cooker. Turn the cooker on, and leave undisturbed until the cooking cycle is complete.

3. Leave the rice in the cooker on the warming cycle to keep hot, and serve.

Braised Beef Round
With Potatoes and Carrots

Top round is one of the leanest beef cuts available. For this recipe, select a top round roast, which may be sold as London broil.

1. Trim any visible fat from the meat. Rinse the meat, and pat it dry with paper towels. Spread the garlic over both sides of the meat, and sprinkle both sides with pepper.

2. Coat a large cast iron skillet or Dutch oven with nonstick cooking spray, and preheat over medium-high heat. Place the meat in the skillet, and brown it for 2 minutes on each side. Remove the skillet from the heat, and spread the onions over the meat. Place the bay leaves and tomato juice in the bottom of the skillet, cover the skillet tightly, and bake at 325°F for 1 hour and 45 minutes.

3. Remove the skillet from the oven, and carefully remove the cover. (Steam will escape.) Place the potatoes and carrots around the meat, cover the skillet tightly, and return it to the oven for another 45 minutes, or until the meat and vegetables are tender. Transfer the meat and vegetables to a serving platter, and keep warm.

4. To make the gravy, discard the bay leaves and pour the meat drippings into a fat separator cup. (If you don't have a separator cup, pour the drippings into a bowl, add a few ice cubes, and skim off the fat once it rises and hardens.) Pour the fat-free drippings into a 2-cup measure, and add enough water to bring the volume up to 1½ cups. Pour the mixture into a 1-quart saucepan, add the bouillon granules, and bring the mixture to a boil over medium heat.

5. Combine the flour and water in a jar with a tight-fitting lid, and shake until smooth. Slowly pour the flour mixture into the boiling gravy. Cook and stir until the gravy is thickened and bubbly.

6. Transfer the gravy to a warmed gravy boat or pitcher, and serve hot with the meat and vegetables.

Yield: 8 servings

2½-pound top round roast or London broil

2 teaspoons crushed fresh garlic

¼ teaspoon coarsely ground black pepper

1 medium yellow onion, thinly sliced

2 bay leaves

½ cup tomato juice

1½ pounds potatoes (about 5 medium), scrubbed and quartered

1¼ pounds carrots (about 6 large), peeled and cut into 2-inch pieces

GRAVY

1½ teaspoons beef bouillon granules

¼ cup unbleached flour

½ cup water

NUTRITIONAL FACTS
(PER SERVING)

Calories: 295	Fiber: 5.1 g
Chol.: 59 mg	Protein: 28 g
Fat: 4.6 g	Sod.: 344 mg

Country-Style Cabbage

Yield: 8 servings

1 large head cabbage (about 2 pounds)

2 tablespoons water

¾ teaspoon chicken bouillon granules

⅛ teaspoon ground black pepper

2 tablespoons cider vinegar

1. Clean and trim the cabbage. Cut the cabbage into quarters, remove the core, and cut each quarter crosswise into 1-inch pieces.

2. Place the water in the bottom of a large skillet or a Dutch oven, and add the cabbage, bouillon granules, and pepper. Cover and cook over medium-low heat, stirring occasionally, for about 15 minutes, or until the cabbage is wilted and tender.

3. Stir in the vinegar, and serve hot.

NUTRITIONAL FACTS (PER ⅔-CUP SERVING)

Calories: 28	Fat: 0.2 g	Protein: 1.5 g
Cholesterol: 0 mg	Fiber: 2.7 g	Sodium: 115 mg

Cinnamon Apples

Yield: 8 servings

½ cup frozen apple juice concentrate, thawed

4 teaspoons cornstarch

8 cups apple slices (about 10 medium)

1 teaspoon ground cinnamon

1. In a small bowl, combine 2 tablespoons of the apple juice concentrate with the cornstarch. Stir to mix, and set aside.

2. Place the apple slices, the remaining apple juice concentrate, and the cinnamon in a 2½-quart pot, and bring the mixture to a boil over high heat. Reduce the heat to low, cover, and simmer, stirring occasionally, for 15 to 20 minutes, or just until the apples are tender.

3. Stir the cornstarch mixture and add to the apple mixture. Cook and stir until the sauce is thickened and clear. Remove from the heat, cool slightly, and serve warm.

NUTRITIONAL FACTS (PER ½-CUP SERVING)

Calories: 97	Fat: 0.4 g	Protein: 0.3 g
Cholesterol: 0 mg	Fiber: 2.2 g	Sodium: 4 mg

Moist Cornmeal Muffins

1. In a large bowl, combine the cornmeal, baking powder, and baking soda, and stir to mix well. Add the egg whites, honey, and buttermilk, and stir just until the dry ingredients are moistened.

2. Coat muffin cups with nonstick cooking spray, and fill ⅔ full with the batter. Bake at 350°F for 15 to 18 minutes, or just until a wooden toothpick inserted in the center of a muffin comes out clean. Be careful not to overbake.

3. Remove the muffin tin from the oven, and allow it to sit for 5 minutes before removing the muffins. Serve warm or at room temperature.

Yield: 12 muffins

2 cups whole grain cornmeal

2 teaspoons baking powder

½ teaspoon baking soda

3 egg whites

2 tablespoons honey

1¾ cups nonfat buttermilk

NUTRITIONAL FACTS (PER MUFFIN)

Calories: 103	Fat: 0.9 g	Protein: 3.7 g
Cholesterol: 0 mg	Fiber: 2 g	Sodium: 148 mg

Fat-Free Carrot Cake
With Creamy Cheese Frosting

Yield: 16 servings

3 cups unbleached flour

1½ cups sugar

2½ teaspoons baking soda

2 teaspoons ground cinnamon

1⅓ cups orange juice

¾ cup fat-free egg substitute

2 teaspoons vanilla extract

4 cups grated carrots (about 8 medium)

½ cup golden raisins or chopped walnuts (optional)

CREAMY CHEESE FROSTING

1 cup nonfat or reduced-fat cream cheese

1½ cups nonfat ricotta cheese

½ cup sugar

1 tablespoon lemon juice

1½ teaspoons vanilla extract

2 tablespoons instant vanilla pudding mix

Far from being junk food, this cake provides almost a whole day's supply of vitamin A in each serving.

1. In a large bowl, combine the flour, sugar, baking soda, and cinnamon, and stir to mix well. Stir in the orange juice, egg substitute, and vanilla extract. Fold in the carrots and the raisins or walnuts if desired.

2. Coat a 9-x-13-inch pan with nonstick cooking spray. Spread the batter evenly in the pan, and bake at 300°F for 50 to 55 minutes, or just until a wooden toothpick inserted in the center of the cake comes out clean. Cool to room temperature.

3. To make the frosting, place all of the frosting ingredients except the pudding mix in the bowl of a food processor, and process until smooth. Add the pudding mix, and process just until the frosting is well mixed.

4. Spread the frosting over the cooled cake. Cut into squares and serve immediately or refrigerate.

NUTRITIONAL FACTS (PER SERVING)

| Calories: 248 | Fat: 0.3 g | Protein: 10 g |
| Cholesterol: 2 mg | Fiber: 1.5 g | Sodium: 261 mg |

Valentine's Day

Want that special someone all to yourself? Set the mood with lovely dishes, linens, flowers, and candlelight, and whip up this simple but elegant Valentine's Day dinner. Then settle in for a romantic evening for two.

Get things started with Spiced Artichoke Spread served with warm French bread and a glass of dry white wine. Next comes a simple Spinach and Mushroom Salad with homemade Sweet and Spicy French Dressing. For the main course, choose from Lemon Scallops Linguine and Glazed Turkey Cutlets With Rice. Paired with Dilled Carrots, either entrée will fill you up without weighing you down. For dessert, this menu offers two delightful options----Poached Pears With Warm Raspberry Sauce and Tiramisu for Two.

With a little planning, this dinner requires minimal last-minute attention. The day before the dinner, prepare Spiced Artichoke Spread just to the point of baking so that you'll be able to pop it into the oven before serving. Rinse the salad greens with cool water, and shake off any excess liquid. Then wrap the greens in paper towels and store them in a covered container or plastic bag in the refrigerator. By making the accompanying dressing at the same time you wash the greens, you'll allow the flavors of the dressing ingredients to mingle.

Both entrées must be prepared directly before serving. Fortunately, both the linguine and the glazed turkey cutlets----as well as the accompanying Dilled Carrots----are a snap to make, and will require little of your time.

If you've chosen to treat your guest of honor to poached pears, poach the fruit a day ahead of time, and refrigerate it so that it will be well chilled by serving time. The raspberry sauce can also be made a day in advance, and then reheated just before serving. If you prefer the Tiramisu, make the dessert several hours before dinner, omitting the whipped topping, and chill the layered confection in its goblets. Before serving, just add a dollop of topping and a sprinkling of cocoa for an impressive dessert that's sure to please.

Valentine's Day Dinner

SERVES 2

Savanah Seafood Spread *(page 28)* with French Bread

Spinach and Mushroom Salad *(page 85)* with
Sweet and Spicy French Dressing *(page 85)*

Lemon Scallops Linguine *(page 86)*
or Glazed Turkey Cutlets With Rice *(page 87)*

Dilled Carrots *(page 88)*

Poached Pears With Warm Raspberry Sauce *(page 89)*
or Tiramisu for Two *(page 90)*

Spinach and Mushroom Salad

1. Divide the spinach between 2 individual salad bowls or plates. Arrange the mushrooms, pepper rings, and garbanzo beans over the lettuce.

2. Serve with Sweet and Spicy French Dressing.

Yield: 2 servings

3½ cups torn spinach leaves

⅓ cup mushroom slices

4 thin rings of red bell pepper

¼ cup drained canned garbanzo beans

NUTRITIONAL FACTS (PER 2-CUP SERVING, SALAD ONLY)

Calories: 60	Fat: 0.8 g	Protein: 5 g
Cholesterol: 0 mg	Fiber: 5 mg	Sodium: 79 mg

Sweet and Spicy French Dressing

1. Place all the ingredients in a blender, and process for 1 minute.

2. Transfer the dressing to a small bowl, cover, and chill before serving.

Yield: ¾ cup

2 tablespoons chopped onion

½ cup apple juice

3 tablespoons white wine vinegar

2 tablespoons tomato paste

1 clove garlic

½ teaspoon paprika

¼ teaspoon chili powder

¼ teaspoon salt

Dash cayenne pepper

NUTRITIONAL FACTS (PER TABLESPOON)

Calories: 8	Fat: 0 g	Protein: 0.1 g
Cholesterol: 0 mg	Fiber: 0.1 g	Sodium: 43 mg

Lemon Scallops Linguine

Yield: 2 servings

4 ounces linguine pasta

1 clove garlic, crushed

8 ounces large uncooked scallops, rinsed and patted dry

1½ cups fresh snow peas

1½ teaspoons minced fresh oregano, or ½ teaspoon dried

SAUCE

¼ cup water

2 tablespoons lemon juice

½ teaspoon chicken bouillon granules

1 teaspoon cornstarch

This delightful dish is equally delicious when made with shrimp.

1. Combine the sauce ingredients in a small bowl, and stir until the cornstarch is dissolved. Set aside.

2. Cook the linguine al dente according to package directions. Drain and set aside.

3. Coat a large nonstick skillet with olive oil cooking spray. Place over medium-high heat, add the garlic and scallops, and stir-fry for a few minutes, until the scallops are nearly opaque. Add the snow peas and oregano, and stir-fry for another couple of minutes, or until the snow peas are crisp-tender and the scallops are done. (Add a tablespoon of water if the skillet becomes too dry.)

4. Reduce the heat to low, add the linguine to the scallop mixture, and toss gently to mix. Stir the sauce ingredients and pour over the linguine. Toss gently until the sauce is thickened and clear. Serve immediately.

NUTRITIONAL FACTS (PER SERVING)

Calories: 345	Fat: 2.1 g	Protein: 28 g
Cholesterol: 37 mg	Fiber: 4.7 g	Sodium: 442 mg

Glazed Turkey Cutlets With Rice

For variety, substitute pork tenderloin medallions for the turkey.

Yield: 2 servings

½ teaspoon crushed fresh garlic

4 turkey breast cutlets, 2 ounces each

1 recipe Broccoli-Rice Pilaf, prepared (below)

GLAZE

2 tablespoons apricot preserves or fruit spread

2 tablespoons orange juice

1½ tablespoons seasoned rice vinegar

1 teaspoon cornstarch

¾ teaspoon fresh rosemary, or ¼ teaspoon dried

1. Combine the glaze ingredients in a small bowl, and stir until the cornstarch is dissolved. Set aside.

2. Coat a large nonstick skillet with cooking spray, and preheat the skillet over medium-high heat. Place the garlic and the turkey cutlets in the skillet, and brown for 2 minutes on each side, or until the meat is no longer pink inside. Transfer the cutlets to a plate and keep warm.

3. Place the skillet over low heat. Stir the glaze mixture, and pour it into the skillet. Cook, stirring constantly, for 30 to 60 seconds, or until the glaze is thickened and bubbly. Add the turkey cutlets to the skillet, and turn them in the glaze until completely coated. Remove the skillet from the heat.

4. Place 1¼ cups of Broccoli-Rice Pilaf on each of 2 dinner plates. Arrange half of the turkey cutlets over each mound of pilaf, and serve immediately.

NUTRITIONAL FACTS (PER SERVING, TURKEY ONLY)

| Calories: 194 | Fat: 1 g | Protein: 26 g |
| Cholesterol: 73 mg | Fiber: 0.3 g | Sodium: 273 mg |

Broccoli-Rice Pilaf

Yield: 2 servings

½ cup uncooked brown rice

1 cup plus 2 tablespoons water or unsalted chicken stock

1 cup fresh broccoli florets

1. Place the rice in a strainer, and rinse under cold running water.

2. Place the rice and the water or chicken stock in a 1-quart pot, and bring to a boil over high heat. Reduce the heat to low, stir the rice, and cover.

3. Allow the rice to simmer, covered, for about 50 minutes, or until the rice is cooked and the liquid has been absorbed. Do not stir the rice while it is cooking, as this can result in sticky rice.

4. Remove the rice from the heat, and let sit, covered, for 5 minutes. Meanwhile, bring a 1-quart pot of water to a boil. Add the broccoli, and boil for about 30 seconds, or just until the broccoli is crisp-tender. Drain the broccoli, stir it into the cooked rice, and serve.

NUTRITIONAL FACTS (PER 1¼-CUP SERVING)

Calories: 183	Fat: 1.5 g	Protein: 5 g
Cholesterol: 0 mg	Fiber: 2.8 g	Sodium: 15 mg

Dilled Carrots

Yield: 2 servings

2 medium-large carrots, diagonally sliced ¼-inch thick

¼ teaspoon sugar

1 tablespoon plus 1½ teaspoons water

1 teaspoon lemon juice

1 teaspoon butter-flavored sprinkles

1½ teaspoons minced fresh dill

1. Place the carrots in a 1-quart pot. In a small bowl, combine the sugar, water, lemon juice, and sprinkles, and pour over the carrots. Cover and place over low heat for 4 to 5 minutes, or until the carrots are tender.

2. Uncover the pot, and cook and stir for 2 minutes, or until most of the water has evaporated.

3. Add the dill and toss to mix well. Serve immediately.

NUTRITIONAL FACTS (PER ⅔-CUP SERVING)

Calories: 29	Fat: 0 g	Protein: 1 g
Cholesterol: 0 mg	Fiber: 2 g	Sodium: 58 mg

Poached Pears
With Warm Raspberry Sauce

Yield: 2 servings

1. Peel the pears, leaving the stems intact.

2. Place the pear nectar in the bottom of a microwave or conventional stove-top steamer, and transfer the pears to the steamer. Cover and cook at high power or over medium-high heat for 4 to 5 minutes, or until tender.

3. Drain the pears, reserving the nectar. Cover the pears and chill for several hours or overnight.

4. To make the sauce, place the cornstarch and sugar in a small saucepan, and stir to mix well. Stir in ⅓ cup of the reserved nectar, and cook and stir over medium-low heat until the mixture is thick and bubbly. Stir in the raspberries, and cook and stir for another minute or 2, or until thick and bubbly.

5. Place the chilled pears in individual serving dishes, and pour the warm sauce over the fruit. Serve immediately.

2 pears

⅓ cup pear nectar

2 teaspoons cornstarch

1 tablespoon plus 1 teaspoon sugar

½ cup fresh or frozen raspberries

NUTRITIONAL FACTS (PER SERVING)

Calories: 180	Fat: 0.8 g	Protein: 1 g
Cholesterol: 0 mg	Fiber: 6.6 g	Sodium: 2 mg

Tiramisu for Two

Yield: 2 servings

¾ cup nonfat ricotta cheese

2 tablespoons confectioners' sugar

¼ teaspoon vanilla extract

1 cup fresh or frozen (thawed) strawberries

1½ teaspoons sugar

2 slices (½-inch each) fat-free pound cake

2 tablespoons plus 2 teaspoons coffee liqueur

¼ cup light whipped topping

¼ teaspoon cocoa powder

1. Combine the ricotta cheese, confectioners' sugar, and vanilla extract in the bowl of a food processor, and process until smooth. Set aside.

2. Combine the strawberries and sugar in a small bowl, and mash them together. Set aside.

3. Crumble 1 piece of the pound cake, and divide it between two 10-ounce balloon wine glasses. In each glass, top the cake with 2 tablespoons of the strawberry mixture, 2 teaspoons of the coffee liqueur, and 3 tablespoons of the ricotta mixture. Repeat the layers. Top each dessert with 2 tablespoons of the light whipped topping, and sprinkle with ⅛ teaspoon of cocoa. Serve immediately.

NUTRITIONAL FACTS (PER SERVING)

Calories: 285	Fat: 1.4 g	Protein: 14 g
Cholesterol: 0 mg	Fiber: 2.1 g	Sodium: 169 mg

Halloween

When the ghosts and goblins have fin- ished making their rounds, lure them in from the chill of an October evening and warm them up with this hot and hearty buffet.

As your guests arrive, greet them with steam- ing mugs of Hot Apple Cider, kept warm and fragrant in a Crock Pot heated casserole or coffee maker. Then bring out warm Fiesta Quesadillas. Garnished with cool and creamy nonfat sour cream, these perfect pick-up meal starters are a favorite of small party-goers and parents alike.

The main course, Two-Bean Chili, is made low in fat with the leanest ground beef avail- able. Or make the chili virtually fat-free by using TVP (texturized vegetable protein) in- stead of beef. Thick and hearty, the vegetarian version of this dish has been known to convert more than a few meat eaters.

Mini Mexican Corn Muffins complement the chili perfectly, and a fresh vegetable platter with Black Olive Dip rounds out the accompani- ments. Moist and fudgy Black Magic Cake with

Fluffy Cocoa Frosting adds the finishing touch to this fuss-free menu.

With a little preparation, this buffet is a breeze. Fiesta Quesadillas are easily assembled ahead of time and baked at the last minute. Two-Bean Chili can be made the day before the party, reheated right before the party begins, and kept warm in a chafing dish. Mini Mexican Corn Muffins, too, can be made ahead, and then reheated as guests arrive. Black Olive Dip tastes even *better* when made in advance, as this allows the flavors to marry and blend, so whip this tempting dip up the day before your party, and chill until serving time. Also cut up the accompanying raw vegetables a day in advance, and keep them crisp and fresh in refrigerated plastic bags or airtight containers. Finally, bake the Black Magic Cake on the morning or afternoon of the party, and refrigerate the dessert until you present it as the crowning touch to a frighteningly good meal.

Halloween Buffet

SERVES 12 TO 14

Hot Apple Cider (page 63)

Fiesta Quesadillas (page 94)

Two-Bean Chili (page 95)

Mini Mexican Corn Muffins (page 96)

*Fresh Vegetable Platter
with Black Olive Dip* (page 52)

Black Magic Cake (page 98)

Hot Apple Cider

For variety, substitute cranberry juice for the apple juice.

Yield: 20 servings

1. Place the water and spices in a large pot, and bring to a boil over high heat. Reduce the heat to low, and simmer for 10 minutes. Strain the mixture, discarding the spices, and return the water to the pot.

2. Add the apple juice to the water, and simmer over low heat until thoroughly heated. Serve warm in mugs.

2 cups water

3 sticks cinnamon

1 tablespoon whole cloves

½ teaspoon whole allspice

2 quarts unsweetened apple juice

NUTRITIONAL FACTS (PER ½-CUP SERVING)

Calories: 46	Fat: 0 g	Protein: 0 g
Cholesterol: 0 mg	Fiber: 0 g	Sodium: 3 mg

Fiesta Quesadillas

Yield: 32 appetizers

¾ cup shredded nonfat or reduced-fat Monterey jack cheese

¾ cup shredded nonfat or reduced-fat Cheddar cheese

8 flour tortillas (8-inch rounds)

½ cup thinly sliced scallions

1 can (4 ounces) chopped green chilies, drained

2–3 tablespoons chopped jalapeño peppers (optional)

1. Combine the cheeses and set aside.

2. Coat a baking sheet with nonstick cooking spray. Brush one side of each tortilla lightly with water. Lay 4 of the tortillas, moist side down, on the baking sheet. Spread ¼ of the cheese mixture on each of the 4 tortillas. Top with ¼ of the scallions, chilies, and jalapeños. Top with the remaining tortillas, placing them moist side up.

3. Bake at 400°F for 7 to 9 minutes, or until the quesadillas are heated through and the cheese is melted. Place the sour cream in a small dish and sprinkle with the scallions. Cut each quesadilla into 8 wedges, transfer to a serving platter, and serve hot, accompanied by the sour cream.

NUTRITIONAL FACTS (PER APPETIZER)

| Calories: 41 | Fat: 0.5 g | Protein: 2.9 g |
| Cholesterol: 1 mg | Fiber: 0.4 g | Sodium: 81 mg |

Variation

To make Fiesta Bean Quesadillas, mash 1 cup of drained canned pinto beans with 1½ teaspoons of chili powder. Divide the beans among the tortillas, and spread evenly. Top with the cheese and the remaining ingredients and bake.

NUTRITIONAL FACTS (PER APPETIZER)

| Calories: 51 | Fat: 0.5 g | Protein: 3.4 g |
| Cholesterol: 1 mg | Fiber: 1 g | Sodium: 93 mg |

Two-Bean Chili

Yield: 16 servings

1. Place the ground beef in a 6-quart stock pot, and brown over medium-high heat, stirring constantly to crumble. Drain off any excess fat.

2. Add the tomatoes, tomato sauce, onion, green pepper, herbs and spices, and bouillon granules to the beef, and stir to mix well. Bring the mixture to a boil over high heat. Then reduce the heat to low, cover the pot, and simmer for 15 minutes.

3. Add the beans to the chili, and stir to mix well. Cover and simmer for 20 minutes. Stir in the vinegar.

4. Transfer the chili to a chafing dish or Crock-Pot heated casserole to keep warm, and serve, topping each serving with grated nonfat Cheddar cheese if desired.

2 pounds 96% lean ground beef

2 cans (1 pound each) unsalted crushed tomatoes

2 cans (1 pound each) unsalted tomato sauce

2 large onions, chopped

2 large green bell peppers, chopped

4–5 tablespoons chili powder

2 teaspoons dried oregano

1 teaspoon ground cumin

2 teaspoons beef bouillon granules

2 cans (1 pound each) kidney beans, drained and rinsed

2 cans (1 pound each) pinto beans, drained and rinsed

3 tablespoons red wine or cider vinegar

2 cups grated nonfat or reduced-fat Cheddar cheese (optional)

NUTRITIONAL FACTS (PER 1-CUP SERVING)

Calories: 191	Fat: 2.6 g	Protein: 15.5 g
Cholesterol: 23 mg	Fiber: 8.9 g	Sodium: 269 mg

Variation

To make Vegetarian Two-Bean Chili, use texturized vegetable protein (TVP)* instead of beef. Just heat 1¾ cups of water and 2 teaspoons of vegetable bouillon granules to the boiling point in a 6-quart stock pot, and stir in 2 cups of TVP. Remove the pot from the heat, and let the mixture sit for 5 minutes, or until all of the liquid has been absorbed. Then add the tomatoes and other ingredients----except the beef bouillon, which is no longer needed----according to the instructions provided above.

NUTRITIONAL FACTS (PER 1-CUP SERVING)

Calories: 171	Fat: 1.2 g	Protein: 13 g
Cholesterol: 0 mg	Fiber: 11.5 g	Sodium: 170 mg

*TVP is a protein-rich alternative to meat. Made from soy flour that has been formed into small nuggets, TVP is cholesterol-free and contains almost no fat. Look for TVP in health foods stores and many grocery stores.

Mini Mexican Corn Muffins

Yield: 24 muffins

1 cup whole wheat flour

1 cup whole grain yellow cornmeal

2 teaspoons baking powder

½ teaspoon baking soda

½ teaspoon whole cumin seeds

1½ cups nonfat buttermilk

2 egg whites

½ cup shredded nonfat or
   reduced-fat Cheddar cheese

1½ tablespoons finely chopped
   jalapeño peppers (optional)

1. Combine the flour, cornmeal, baking powder, baking soda, and cumin seeds in a large bowl, and stir to mix well. Add the buttermilk and egg whites, and stir just until the dry ingredients are moistened. Fold in the cheese and, if desired, the jalapeño peppers.

2. Coat mini-muffin tins with nonstick cooking spray, and fill each cup *completely full* with the batter. Bake at 350°F for about 10 minutes, or just until a wooden toothpick inserted in the center of a muffin comes out clean. Be careful not to overbake.

3. Remove the muffins tins from the oven, and allow them to sit for 5 minutes before removing the muffins. Serve warm.

NUTRITIONAL FACTS (PER MUFFIN)

Calories: 41	Fat: 0.2 g	Protein: 2.1 g
Cholesterol: 0 mg	Fiber: 1.1 g	Sodium: 67 mg

Black Olive Dip

1. Combine the ingredients in a medium-sized bowl. Transfer the dip to a serving dish, cover, and chill for at least 2 hours.

2. Serve with fat-free tortilla chips, celery sticks, and carrot sticks.

Yield: 2¾ cups

2 cups nonfat sour cream

½ cup chopped black olives

¼ cup finely chopped scallions

NUTRITIONAL FACTS (PER TABLESPOON)

Calories: 13	Fat: 0.2 g	Protein: 0.7 g
Cholesterol: 0 mg	Fiber: 0.1 g	Sodium: 27 mg

Black Magic Cake

Yield: 16 servings

2¼ cups unbleached flour

¾ cup oat flour

1½ cups sugar

½ cup cocoa powder

2 teaspoons baking soda

¼ teaspoon salt (optional)

2 cups water

¼ cup plus 2 tablespoons prepared coffee, cooled to room temperature

1 tablespoon cider vinegar

2 teaspoons vanilla extract

FLUFFY COCOA FROSTING

¾ cup sugar

¼ cup light corn syrup

¼ cup water

3 large egg whites, warmed to room temperature

1 teaspoon vanilla extract

1 tablespoon cocoa powder

NUTRITIONAL FACTS (PER SERVING)

Calories: 216   Fiber: 2 g
Chol.: 0 mg   Protein: 3.2 g
Fat: 1 g   Sod.: 129 mg

---

1. In a large bowl, combine the flours, sugar, cocoa, baking soda, and salt, if desired, and stir to mix well. In a small bowl, combine the water, coffee, vinegar, and vanilla extract. Add the coffee mixture to the flour mixture, and stir to mix well.

2. Coat a 9-x-13-inch pan with nonstick cooking spray. Pour the batter into the pan, and bake at 350°F for 30 to 35 minutes, or just until the top springs back when lightly touched and a wooden toothpick inserted in the center of the cake comes out clean. Be careful not to overbake. Cool the cake to room temperature.

3. To make the frosting, place the sugar, corn syrup, and water in a small, heavy saucepan. Stir until the sugar dissolves. Place the saucepan over medium heat, and bring to a boil. Continue boiling the mixture without stirring until the temperature reaches 240°F on a candy thermometer, or until a drop of syrup forms a soft ball in cold water.

4. Just before the temperature of the syrup reaches 240°F, place the egg whites in the bowl of an electric mixer, and beat until the whites form soft peaks. Add the hot syrup in a slow, thin stream while beating at high speed. Continue beating for 3 to 5 minutes, or until the icing is glossy and firm enough to spread. Beat in the vanilla extract. Finally, beat in the cocoa 1 teaspoonful at a time.

5. Immediately spread the frosting evenly over the cake. Cut into squares, and serve immediately or refrigerate.

Variation

Instead of baking the cake in one large pan, use two 9-inch round pans, and bake for only 25 minutes. Cool the cakes in the pans, and invert one layer upside down onto a serving platter. Spread the cake with a layer of icing, and top it with the second layer, placing it right side up. Complete the layer cake by frosting the sides and top, swirling the frosting with a spoon or knife.

Part Four

Festive Fat-Free Desserts and Treats

The holidays bring an abundance of delicious desserts and baked goods, some of which are unavailable at any other time of year. These sweet and savory treats are the stars of holiday parties, and are often given as gifts, as well. At other times of the year, of course, breads, muffins, and desserts are just as welcome. A spicy fruit crisp, super-moist cake, or fruit-filled bread adds that special touch to any get-together, whether an elaborate sit-down affair or a backyard barbecue.

The recipes presented in this section----as well as in the holiday and party menus found in Parts Two and Three ----will allow you to serve healthful no-fat treats which taste so great, no one but you will guess just how wholesome they are. These recipes contain no butter, margarine, oil, or shortening of any kind. Instead, ingredients like fruit purées, juices, nonfat yogurt, nonfat buttermilk, and liquid sweeteners add moistness, eliminating the need for fat. In addition, these recipes contain less sugar than most dessert recipes do. Fruits and fruit juices, flavorings like vanilla extract and cinnamon, and mildly sweet flours like oat have been used to reduce the need for sugar, and to add fiber and other nutrients, as well.

Before taking out your baking pans and preheating your oven, you might wish to turn to "Getting the Fat Out of Parties," on page 3. That section will acquaint you with the whole grain flours you'll be using, and will guide you in substituting less-refined sweeteners for traditional sweeteners, if you wish to do so. Then get ready to create some of the healthiest and best-tasting desserts and snacks you've ever tasted. Even if you're short on time, these simple, easy-to-follow recipes will help make your next special-occasion gathering an event to remember.

Making Prune Purée and Prune Butter

The dessert recipes in this book use a variety of fat substitutes, including fruit purées, fruit juices, applesauce, and nonfat buttermilk. Most of these substitutes are readily available in grocery stores. Two excellent fat substitutes, however, must be made at home. Prune Purée and Prune Butter will allow you to make moist and flavorful baked goods with little or no fat, and will add fiber and nutrients as well. Simply follow the recipes provided below, and keep these ingredients on hand for use in many holiday recipes.

Prune Purée

Yield: 1½ cups

3 ounces pitted prunes (about ½ cup)

1 cup water or fruit juice

2 teaspoons lecithin granules*

1. Place all ingredients in a blender or food processor, and process at high speed until the mixture is smooth.

2. Use immediately, or place in an airtight container and store for up to 3 weeks in the refrigerator.

Prune Butter

Yield: 1 cup

8 ounces pitted prunes (about 1⅓ cups)

6 tablespoons water or fruit juice

1. Place both ingredients in a food processor, and process at high speed until the mixture is a smooth paste. (Note that this mixture is too thick to be made in a blender.)

2. Use immediately, or place in an airtight container and store for up to 3 weeks in the refrigerator.

Orange Date Bread

Yield: 15 slices

1 cup orange juice
¾ cup chopped dates
1½ cups whole wheat flour
2 tablespoons sugar
1 teaspoon baking soda
1 teaspoon baking powder
1 teaspoon vanilla extract
¼ cup chopped walnuts (optional)

1. Place the orange juice in a small saucepan, and bring to a boil over high heat. Place the dates in a small bowl, and pour the orange juice over the dates. Set aside to cool.

2. In a large bowl, combine the flour, sugar, baking soda, and baking powder, and stir to mix well. Stir the vanilla extract into the cooled date mixture, add the date mixture to the flour mixture, and stir just until the dry ingredients are moistened. Fold in the walnuts if desired.

3. Coat a 7½-x-3¾-inch loaf pan with nonstick cooking spray. Spread the batter evenly in the pan, and bake at 350°F for about 30 minutes, or just until a wooden toothpick inserted in the center of the loaf comes out clean.

4. Remove the bread from the oven, and let sit for 10 minutes. Invert the loaf onto a wire rack, turn right side up, and cool to room temperature before slicing and serving.

NUTRITIONAL FACTS (PER SLICE)

Calories: 79   Fiber: 2.3 g
Cholesterol: 0 mg Protein: 2 g
Fat: 0.3 g   Sodium: 78 mg

Cranberry Applesauce Bread

Yield: 16 slices

1 cup unsweetened applesauce

½ cup quick-cooking oats

1⅔ cups whole wheat flour

½ cup sugar

1 teaspoon baking soda

1 teaspoon baking powder

½ teaspoon ground cinnamon

2 egg whites

¾ cup coarsely chopped fresh or frozen cranberries (do not thaw)

1. In a small bowl, combine the applesauce and oats. Set aside for 5 minutes.

2. In a large bowl, combine the flour, sugar, baking soda, baking powder, and cinnamon, and stir to mix well. Add the applesauce mixture and the egg whites to the flour mixture, and stir just until the dry ingredients are moistened. Fold in the cranberries.

3. Coat an 8-x-4-inch loaf pan with nonstick cooking spray. Spread the batter evenly in the pan, and bake at 350°F for about 45 minutes, or just until a wooden toothpick inserted in the center of the loaf comes out clean.

4. Remove the bread from the oven, and let sit for 10 minutes. Invert the loaf onto a wire rack, turn right side up, and cool to room temperature before slicing and serving.

NUTRITIONAL FACTS (PER SLICE)

Calories: 87	Fat: 0.4 g	Protein: 2.6 g
Cholesterol: 0 mg	Fiber: 2.1 g	Sodium: 109 mg

Whole Wheat Apricot Bread

1. Place the apricots in a small bowl, and pour the boiling water over the apricots. Stir in the honey, and set aside to cool.

2. In a large bowl, combine the flour, baking soda, and baking powder, and stir to mix well. Add the cooled apricot mixture and the milk, Prune Purée, and vanilla extract to the flour mixture, and stir just until the dry ingredients are moistened. Fold in the granola.

3. Coat two 5¾-x-3¼-inch loaf pans with nonstick cooking spray, and divide the batter evenly between the pans. Bake at 325°F for about 30 minutes, or just until a wooden toothpick inserted in the center of a loaf comes out clean.

4. Remove the bread from the oven, and let sit for 10 minutes. Invert the loaves onto a wire rack, turn right side up, and cool to room temperature before slicing and serving.

Yield: 20 slices

1 cup chopped dried apricots

½ cup boiling water

¼ cup plus 2 tablespoons honey

2 cups whole wheat flour

¼ teaspoon baking soda

2 teaspoons baking powder

¼ cup evaporated skim milk

¼ cup plus 2 tablespoons Prune Purée (page 100)

1 teaspoon vanilla extract

¾ cup nonfat or low-fat granola cereal

NUTRITIONAL FACTS (PER SLICE)

Calories: 89	Fat: 0.2 g	Protein: 2.3 g
Cholesterol: 0 mg	Fiber: 2.3 g	Sodium: 71 mg

Fresh Pear Bread

Yield: 16 slices

2 cups whole wheat flour

½ cup sugar

1 teaspoon baking soda

1 teaspoon baking powder

¼ teaspoon ground nutmeg

¼ teaspoon ground cinnamon

¾ cup pear nectar

1⅓ cups finely chopped fresh pear (about 1½ medium)

¼ cup currants or dark raisins

1. In a large bowl, combine the flour, sugar, baking soda, baking powder, nutmeg, and cinnamon, and stir to mix well. Add the pear nectar and chopped pear, and stir just until the dry ingredients are moistened. Fold in the currants or raisins.

2. Coat an 8-x-4-inch loaf pan with cooking spray. Spread the batter in the pan, and bake at 350°F for 45 minutes, or until a wooden toothpick inserted comes out clean.

3. Remove the bread from the oven, and let sit for 10 minutes. Invert the loaf onto a wire rack, turn right side up, and cool to room temperature before slicing and serving.

NUTRITIONAL FACTS (PER SLICE)
Calories: 98   Fat: 0.3 g   Protein: 2.2 g
Cholesterol: 0 mg   Fiber: 2.4 g   Sodium: 75 mg

Pumpkin Spice Bread

Yield: 16 slices

2 cups whole wheat flour

½ cup light brown sugar

1 teaspoon baking soda

1 teaspoon baking powder

1½ teaspoons pumpkin pie spice

¾ cup plus 2 tablespoons orange juice

½ cup mashed cooked or canned pumpkin

1 egg white

⅓ cup dried cranberries or chopped pecans (optional)

1. In a large bowl, combine the flour, sugar, baking soda, baking powder, and pumpkin pie spice, and stir to mix well. Add the juice, pumpkin, and egg white, and stir just until the dry ingredients are moistened. Fold in the cranberries or pecans if desired.

2. Coat an 8-x-4-inch loaf pan with cooking spray. Spread the batter in the pan, and bake at 350°F for 40 minutes, or until a wooden toothpick inserted in the center comes out clean.

3. Remove the bread from the oven, and let sit for 10 minutes. Invert the loaf onto a wire rack, turn right side up, and cool to room temperature before slicing and serving.

NUTRITIONAL FACTS (PER SLICE)
Calories: 78   Fat: 0.3 g   Protein: 2.5 g.
Cholesterol: 0 mg   Fiber: 2.1 g   Sodium: 108 mg

Harvest Pumpkin Muffins

1. To make the topping, combine the brown sugar and wheat germ in a small bowl. Set aside.

2. In a large bowl, combine the flour, brown sugar, baking powder, and pumpkin pie spice, and stir to mix well. Add the pumpkin, apple juice, and egg whites, and stir just until the dry ingredients are moistened. Fold in the apple.

3. Coat muffin cups with nonstick cooking spray, and fill ¾ full with the batter. Sprinkle the topping over the batter, and bake at 350°F for 16 to 18 minutes, or just until a wooden toothpick inserted in the center of a muffin comes out clean.

4. Remove the muffin tin from the oven, and allow it to sit for 5 minutes before removing the muffins. Serve warm or at room temperature.

Yield: 12 muffins

2 cups whole wheat flour

½ cup light brown sugar

1 tablespoon plus 1 teaspoon baking powder

1¼ teaspoons pumpkin pie spice

⅔ cup mashed cooked or canned pumpkin

½ cup plus 1 tablespoon apple juice

2 egg whites

1¼ cups finely chopped apple (about 1½ medium)

TOPPING

1 tablespoon light brown sugar

1 tablespoon toasted wheat germ

NUTRITIONAL FACTS (PER MUFFIN)

Calories: 116	Fat: 0.5 g	Protein: 3.5 g
Cholesterol: 0 mg	Fiber: 3 g	Sodium: 135 mg

Holiday Banana Muffins

Yield: 12 muffins

2 cups whole wheat flour

¼ cup light brown sugar

1 tablespoon baking powder

1 cup mashed very ripe banana
(about 2 large)

⅓ cup orange juice

2 egg whites

1 teaspoon vanilla extract

⅓ cup dried cranberries or golden
raisins

TOPPING

1 tablespoon light brown sugar

1 tablespoon finely ground pecans

1. To make the topping, combine the brown sugar and pecans in a small bowl. Set aside.

2. In a large bowl, combine the flour, brown sugar, and baking powder, and stir to mix well. Add the banana, orange juice, egg whites, and vanilla extract, and stir just until the dry ingredients are moistened. Fold in the cranberries or raisins.

3. Coat muffin cups with nonstick cooking spray, and fill ¾ full with the batter. Sprinkle the topping over the batter, and bake at 350°F for 14 to 16 minutes, or just until a wooden toothpick inserted in the center of a muffin comes out clean.

4. Remove muffin tin from oven, and allow it to sit for 5 minutes before removing muffins. Serve warm or at room temperature.

NUTRITIONAL FACTS (PER MUFFIN)

Calories: 131	Fat: 0.9 g	Protein: 3.8 g
Cholesterol: 0 mg	Fiber: 3.1 g	Sodium: 95 mg

Apple Butter Bran Muffins

Yield: 12 muffins

1 cup whole wheat flour

1 cup wheat bran

½ cup oat bran

1 teaspoon baking soda

½ teaspoon ground cinnamon

1 cup apple butter

1 cup nonfat buttermilk

2 egg whites

½ cup dark raisins

1. Combine the flour, wheat bran, oat bran, baking soda, and cinnamon, and stir to mix well. Add the apple butter, buttermilk, and egg whites, and stir just until the dry ingredients are moistened. Fold in the raisins.

2. Coat muffin cups with cooking spray, and fill ¾ full with batter. Bake at 350°F for 15 to 18 minutes, or until a wooden toothpick inserted in the center comes out clean.

3. Remove muffin tin from oven, and allow it to sit for 5 minutes before removing muffins. Serve warm or at room temperature.

NUTRITIONAL FACTS (PER MUFFIN)

Calories: 123	Fat: 0.9 g	Protein: 4.1 g
Cholesterol: 0 mg	Fiber: 3.8 g	Sodium: 101 mg

Lebkuchen

These chewy spice cookies are a traditional German holiday treat.

Yield: 34 cookies

1. In a large bowl, combine the flours, brown sugar, baking soda, spices, and orange rind, and stir to mix well. Add the honey and orange juice, and stir to mix well. Add the almonds and dried fruit, and stir to mix.

2. Coat a baking sheet with nonstick cooking spray. Roll the dough into 1-inch balls, and place 1½ inches apart on the baking sheet. Using the bottom of a glass dipped in sugar, flatten the cookies to ¼-inch thickness.

3. Bake at 275°F for about 18 minutes, or until golden brown. Cool the cookies on the pan for 1 minute. Then transfer the cookies to wire racks, and cool completely. Serve immediately, or transfer to an airtight container, and arrange in single layers separated by sheets of waxed paper.

1 cup whole wheat flour

¾ cup unbleached flour

¼ cup plus 2 tablespoons brown sugar

¾ teaspoon baking soda

¾ teaspoon ground cinnamon

¼ teaspoon ground nutmeg

¼ teaspoon ground cloves

½ teaspoon dried grated orange rind

¼ cup plus 2 tablespoons honey

3 tablespoons plus 2 teaspoons orange juice

¼ cup finely chopped almonds

⅓ cup finely chopped mixed dried fruit

NUTRITIONAL FACTS (PER COOKIE)

Calories: 50	Fat: 0.6 g	Protein: 1.0 g
Cholesterol: 0 mg	Fiber: 0.7 g	Sodium: 29 mg

Peppermint Brownies

Yield: 36 servings

4 squares (1 ounce each) unsweetened baking chocolate

1½ cups sugar

½ cup plus 1 tablespoon egg substitute

¾ cup Prune Butter (page 108)

2 teaspoons vanilla extract

1½ cups unbleached flour

¼ teaspoon salt (optional)

½ cup skim milk

¾ cup chopped walnuts (optional)

GLAZE

1 cup confectioners' sugar

1 teaspoon vanilla extract

4 drops peppermint extract

2 drops green food coloring

4–5 teaspoons skim milk

1. If using a microwave oven to melt the chocolate, place the chocolate in a small bowl and microwave uncovered at high power for 3 to 4 minutes, or until almost melted. Remove the bowl from the oven and stir the chocolate until completely melted. If melting the chocolate on the stove top, place the chocolate in a small saucepan and cook over low heat, stirring constantly, until melted.

2. Place the melted chocolate in a large bowl, and stir in first the sugar, and then the egg substitute, Prune Butter, and vanilla extract. Stir to mix well. Stir in the flour, the salt, if desired, and the milk. Fold in the walnuts if desired.

3. Coat a 9-x-13-inch pan with nonstick cooking spray. Spread the batter evenly in the pan, and bake at 325°F for 35 to 40 minutes, or just until the center springs back when lightly touched. Be careful not to overbake. Cool to room temperature.

4. To make the glaze, combine the glaze ingredients in a small bowl. If using a microwave oven, microwave the glaze uncovered at high power for 20 seconds, or until runny. If using a conventional stove top, transfer the glaze to a small saucepan and place over medium heat for 30 seconds, stirring constantly. Drizzle the glaze over the brownies, and let harden before cutting into squares and serving.

NUTRITIONAL FACTS (PER SERVING)

Calories: 99	Fat: 1.5 g	Protein: 1.6 g
Cholesterol: 0 mg	Fiber: 1.3 g	Sodium: 28 mg

Mocha Carrot Cake

Yield: 16 servings

1. In a large bowl, combine the flour, sugar, cocoa, and baking soda, and stir to mix well. Add the coffee, egg whites, and vanilla extract, and stir to mix well. Stir in the carrots, the raisins, and, if desired, the walnuts.

2. Coat a 9-x-13-inch pan with nonstick cooking spray, and spread the batter evenly in the pan. Bake at 325°F for about 40 minutes, or just until a wooden toothpick inserted in the center of the cake comes out clean. Cool to room temperature.

3. To make the icing, place the cream cheese and ricotta in a food processor or blender, and process until smooth. Add the confectioners' sugar and vanilla extract, and process to mix well. Spread the icing over the cooled cake, and serve immediately or refrigerate.

2 cups unbleached flour

1¼ cups sugar

½ cup cocoa powder

2 teaspoons baking soda

¾ cup plus 2 tablespoons coffee, cooled to room temperature

4 egg whites

2 teaspoons vanilla extract

3 cups grated carrots (about 6 medium)

½ cup dark raisins

½ cup chopped walnuts (optional)

CREAM CHEESE ICING

1 cup nonfat or reduced-fat cream cheese

1 cup nonfat ricotta cheese

½ cup confectioners' sugar

1 teaspoon vanilla extract

NUTRITIONAL FACTS (PER SERVING)

Calories: 192	Fat: 0.7 g	Protein: 8.3 g
Cholesterol: 0 mg	Fiber: 2.2 g	Sodium: 237 mg

Applesauce Gingerbread

Yield: 16 servings

1½ cups unbleached flour

1 cup whole wheat flour

⅔ cup sugar

2½ teaspoons baking soda

1 teaspoon ground ginger

1 teaspoon ground cinnamon

1 teaspoon ground allspice

1½ cups unsweetened applesauce

1 cup molasses

3 egg whites

1½ cups light whipped topping (optional)

1. In a large bowl, combine the flours, sugar, baking soda, and spices, and stir to mix well. Add the applesauce, molasses, and egg whites, and stir to mix well.

2. Coat a 9-x-13-inch pan with cooking spray, and spread the batter in the pan. Bake at 325°F for 40 minutes, or just until a wooden toothpick inserted in the center comes out clean.

3. Cool the cake to room temperature, cut into squares, and serve, topping each serving with a dollop of light whipped topping, if desired.

NUTRITIONAL FACTS (PER SERVING)

Calories: 157	Fat: 0.3 g	Protein: 3.1 g
Cholesterol: 0 mg	Fiber: 1.6 g	Sodium: 146 mg

Pear-Maple Crisp

Yield: 6 servings

FRUIT FILLING

6 cups sliced fresh pears (about 6 medium)

1 tablespoon cornstarch

¼ teaspoon ground cinnamon

2 tablespoons maple syrup

¼ cup dark raisins or chopped walnuts (optional)

TOPPING

½ cup quick-cooking oats

3 tablespoons whole wheat flour

3 tablespoons light brown sugar

2 tablespoons maple syrup

1. To make the topping, combine the oats, flour, and brown sugar in a small bowl, and stir to mix. Add the maple syrup, and stir until the mixture is moist and crumbly. Set aside.

2. In a large bowl, combine the pears, cornstarch, and cinnamon, and toss to mix well. Drizzle the maple syrup over the pears, and toss gently. Toss in the raisins or walnuts if desired. Place the mixture in a 9-inch deep dish pie pan, and sprinkle with the topping.

3. Bake at 350°F for 35 to 40 minutes, or until the filling is bubbly and the topping is nicely browned. If the topping starts to brown too quickly, cover the dish loosely with aluminum foil during the last 10 minutes of baking. Serve warm.

NUTRITIONAL FACTS (PER SERVING)

Calories: 185	Fat: 0.9 g	Protein: 2.1 g
Cholesterol: 0 mg	Fiber: 4.8 g	Sodium: 4 mg

Mini Cherry Cheesecakes

If you are unable to locate fat-free graham crackers, just use regular graham crackers. They, too, are low in fat.

1. Break the crackers into pieces, and place in the bowl of a food processor or in a blender. Process into fine crumbs. Measure the crumbs. There should be 1¼ cups. (Adjust the amount if necessary.)

2. Return the crumbs to the food processor, and add the sugar and egg substitute. Process until the mixture resembles moist crumbs.

3. Coat nonstick mini-muffin tins with nonstick cooking spray. Place 1½ teaspoons of the graham cracker mixture in the bottom of each muffin cup, and use a pastry press or small spoon to push the mixture over the bottom and ¼ inch up the sides of each cup. (Periodically dip the pastry press or spoon in sugar to prevent sticking).

4. Bake the crusts at 350°F for 5 to 6 minutes, or until they feel firm and dry. Remove from the oven and set aside to cool.

5. Place all of the filling ingredients in a food processor or blender, and process until smooth. Place 1 tablespoon of filling in each graham cracker shell, and bake at 300°F for 25 minutes, or until the filling is puffed and lightly browned around the edges. Turn the oven off, and let the cheesecakes cool in the oven with the door ajar for 1 hour.

6. Top each cheesecake with 1 teaspoon of cherry filling. Chill for several hours or overnight before serving.

Yield: 40 servings

CRUST

8 large (2½-x-5-inch) fat-free graham crackers

2 tablespoons sugar

2 tablespoons fat-free egg substitute

FILLING

1½ cups nonfat or reduced-fat cream cheese

1 cup dry curd or nonfat cottage cheese

½ cup fat-free egg substitute

½ cup sugar

2½ tablespoons unbleached flour

2 teaspoons vanilla extract

TOPPING

¾ cup plus 2 tablespoons canned light (low-sugar) cherry pie filling

NUTRITIONAL FACTS (PER SERVING)

| Calories: 45 | Fat: 0.3 g | Protein: 3.1 g |
| Cholesterol: 2 mg | Fiber: 0.2 g | Sodium: 89 mg |

Cranberry Upside-Down Cake

Yield: 9 servings

2 tablespoons frozen orange juice concentrate, thawed

1 tablespoon water

⅓ cup brown sugar

1 cup plus 2 tablespoons fresh or frozen cranberries (do not thaw)

1¼ cups unbleached flour

⅓ cup oat flour

1½ teaspoons baking powder

½ cup sugar

⅔ cup skim milk

⅓ cup honey

2 egg whites

1 teaspoon vanilla extract

While this cake is baking, the cranberries float up into the batter, leaving an orange glaze that forms a festive topping when the cake is turned upside down.

1. Coat an 8-inch square pan with nonstick cooking spray. Combine the orange juice concentrate and water in a small bowl, and spread the mixture over the bottom of the pan. Sprinkle the brown sugar over the concentrate, and arrange the cranberries over the sugar. Set aside.

2. In a large bowl, combine the flours, baking powder, and sugar, and stir to mix well. Add the milk, honey, egg whites, and vanilla extract, and stir to mix well. Pour the batter over the cranberries.

3. Bake at 350°F for 35 to 40 minutes, or just until a wooden toothpick inserted in the center of the cake comes out clean. Loosen the sides of the cake by running a knife around each edge, and *immediately* invert onto a serving platter. If any glaze remains in the pan, spread the glaze over the top of the cake. Let sit for at least 20 minutes before cutting into squares and serving.

NUTRITIONAL FACTS (PER SERVING)

Calories: 210	Fat: 0.4 g	Protein: 4 g
Cholesterol: 0 mg	Fiber: 1.4 g	Sodium: 110 mg

Chocolate-Almond Cannoli Cake

This cake is made in a flan or tiara pan. The bottom of the pan has a raised center that makes an ideal place to put the filling after the cake has been baked, cooled, and inverted.

1. In a large bowl, combine the flours, sugar, cocoa, baking soda, and salt, if desired, and stir to mix well. In a small bowl, combine the water, vinegar, liqueur, and vanilla extract. Add the vinegar mixture to the flour mixture, and stir to mix well.

2. Coat a 10-inch flan pan with nonstick cooking spray. Spread the batter evenly in the pan, and bake at 350°F for about 15 minutes, or just until a wooden toothpick inserted in the center of the cake comes out clean. Let the cake cool to room temperature in the pan. Then invert onto a serving platter.

3. To make the filling, place the ricotta cheese, confectioners' sugar, and almond extract in the bowl of a food processor or in a blender, and process until smooth. (Do not add more sugar, as this will make the filling too thin.) Fill the depression in the top of the cake with the filling. Arrange the strawberries around the edge of the filling and, if desired, sprinkle the almonds over the top.

4. Chill the cake for several hours, cut into wedges, and serve.

Yield: 10 servings

1 cup unbleached flour

½ cup oat flour

½ cup plus 2 tablespoons sugar

¼ cup cocoa powder

1 teaspoon baking soda

⅛ teaspoon salt (optional)

1 cup water

1½ teaspoons white wine or cider vinegar

¼ cup amaretto liqueur

1 teaspoon vanilla extract

FILLING

15 ounces nonfat ricotta cheese

⅓ cup confectioners' sugar

½ teaspoon almond extract

2 cups sliced fresh strawberries

2 tablespoons toasted sliced almonds (optional)

NUTRITIONAL FACTS (PER SERVING)

Calories: 198	Fat: 0.6 g	Protein: 8.6 g
Cholesterol: 0 mg	Fiber: 2.5 g	Sodium: 158 mg

Fresh Fruit Trifle

Yield: 12 servings

1 fat-free pound or angel food cake (12 ounces)

⅓ cup raspberry jam or fruit spread

1 tablespoon amaretto or chambord liqueur

4 cups mixed fresh fruit

3 cups vanilla pudding made with skim milk

TOPPING

1 cup light whipped topping

1 cup nonfat vanilla yogurt

1 cup mixed fresh fruit (optional)

Use your choice of seasonal fresh fruit to make this beautiful layered dessert. Strawberries, kiwis, bananas, peaches, raspberries, blueberries, and seedless green grapes all yield delicious results.

1. Slice the cake into ¾-inch slices, and spread each piece with jam on one side. Set aside.

2. Drizzle the liqueur over the sides and bottom of a 3-quart trifle bowl or other decorative glass bowl. Arrange half of the cake slices over the bottom of the bowl. Top with half of the fruit, and then half of the pudding. Repeat the cake, fruit, and pudding layers.

3. Place the whipped topping in a small bowl, and fold the yogurt into the topping. Swirl the mixture over the top of the trifle, and garnish with fresh fruit, if desired. Cover and chill for at least 2 hours before serving.

NUTRITIONAL FACTS (PER 1-CUP SERVING)

Calories: 209	Fat: 1 g	Protein: 5.5 g
Cholesterol: 0 mg	Fiber: 1.5 g	Sodium: 165 mg